DIVINE COMMAND MORALITY

For my father, Hugh Joseph Rooney

Divine Command Morality

PAUL ROONEY

Avebury
Aldershot • Brookfield USA • Hong Kong • Singapore • Sydney

© Paul Rooney 1996

All rights reserved. No part of this publication may be reproduced, stored in a retrieval system, or transmitted in any form or by any means, electronic, mechanical, photocopying, recording or otherwise without the prior permission of the publisher.

Published by
Avebury
Ashgate Publishing Ltd
Gower House
Croft Road
Aldershot
Hants GU11 3HR
England

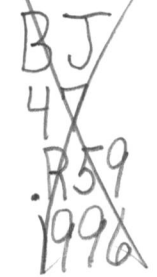

Ashgate Publishing Company
Old Post Road
Brookfield
Vermont 05036
USA

British Library Cataloguing in Publication Data

Rooney, Paul
    Divine command morality. - (Avebury series in philosophy)
    1. Christian ethics 2. Religion - Philosophy 3. God
    I. Title
    241.2

    ISBN 1 85972 505 8

Library of Congress Catalog Card Number: 96-78638

Printed and bound by Athenaeum Press, Ltd.,
Gateshead, Tyne & Wear.

Contents

Acknowledgements vi

1 Introduction 1

2 Morality and religion 7

3 Autonomy, obedience and power 28

4 Natural law, reason and conscience 48

5 Christian Platonism and God's nature 75

6 Arbitrary commands 97

7 Conclusion 115

Bibliography 123

Acknowledgements

Versions of some chapters have been published previously under the following titles: 'Divine commands, natural law and Aquinas', *Scottish Journal of Religious Studies*, 1995 (chapter four); 'Divine commands, Christian Platonism and God's nature', *The Heythrop Journal*, 1996, Basil Blackwell Ltd. (chapter five); 'Divine commands and arbitrariness', *Religious Studies*, 1995, Cambridge University Press (chapter six); 'Literalism and tolerance', *New Blackfriars*, 1995 (parts of the conclusion). I am grateful to Professor S.R.L. Clark, Michael Durrant, Professor Paul Helm and Dr N.M.L. Nathan for their useful comments. Thanks are due in particular to Dr John Joseph Downes for his assistance and encouragement.

1 Introduction

Content and structure

Suppose that someone asks why one should not commit murder. The reply of the divine command theorist, citing scripture, is 'Because God has forbidden it'. Suppose further that God has indeed forbidden it, and that the questioner responds along the following lines: 'But is it not because it is wrong that one should avoid it? Has not God only forbidden it because it is wrong? Can we not see that it is wrong without God telling us? Would not God have to forbid it, given His traditionally accepted nature?' In each case, the divine command theorist replies (with, perhaps, some qualification), 'No'. And to a final question, 'Then are God's commands arbitrary?', the reply is 'Yes'.

This book is a philosophical defence of the tenability of divine command theory as an acceptable Christian account of morality. The theory states that morality is founded upon God's commands. It has been associated particularly with Duns Scotus and William of Ockham. What God commands, man has a moral duty to do; what He forbids, man ought to avoid; and man's duties arise only because God commands or forbids certain things. There are various ways of understanding what constitutes a divine command, but what I have in mind is chiefly the claim that revealed, scriptural commands are the foundation of morality. Accordingly I propose to explain and justify in this context those replies, just mentioned, of the divine command theorist.

A distinction is sometimes drawn, by those who accept that God determines what is good and what is bad, between the function of God's will and the function of His commands. It may be held, then, that it is ultimately God's will, and not His command, that determines moral principles. I shall defend the view that we can not know His will without knowing what He has commanded, and that divine commands are indeed foundational to morality. The sense in which this is so, and what is the role of His will as against His command, will become clear as the argument progresses.

The structure of the book is roughly as follows. In chapter two I consider whether we can know that God's commands are good if we do not already have knowledge of what is good - whether, therefore, goodness (or the knowledge of it) must be independent of God; I also discuss here an objection to divine command theory which arises from the logical analysis of the meaning of 'good'. Chapter three is concerned with the question whether, if we do not have an independently grounded idea of goodness, we abandon our moral autonomy when we obey God. Chapter four concerns the Christian opposition to divine command theory which stems from the conviction that we can reason out our duties without recourse to revealed commands. In the fifth chapter I examine arguments that morality is such that God would have to command or forbid certain things, because of His nature and the nature of goodness. The arguments of these chapters lead, if successful, to the conclusion that morality is arbitrary; this is the subject of the sixth chapter.

The objections which I discuss are, in the main, ones which are aimed at showing that the theory is logically flawed or logically irreconcilable with the tradition. My arguments, therefore, are principally intended to show that the position put forward is a logical possibility. But I hope to show more than that. One may acknowledge a position as a logical possibility but still hold that there is absolutely no reason to accept it; or one might insist that one could not even imagine what would count as grounds for believing in it. That is to say, one might accept that it was logical, that it was internally consistent and consistent with known facts about the world, but not that it was rational, where rationality (or reasonableness) was narrower in scope than bare logical coherence. For this reason, some of my arguments are directed towards establishing a stronger claim: towards the end of the work I offer an account of the way in which divine command theory can be made more plausible than might be conceded, at first sight, by its opponents.

The context of the argument

The arguments over divine command theory take place against a background which contains two prominent features: first, widely held beliefs about the nature of any moral system (whether religious or not), and second, religious beliefs about the nature of God and goodness. The discussion in the two chapters which follow is conducted more with the first feature in mind, and that of the remaining chapters with more reference to the second. But throughout the book the religious background assumed is that of a fairly orthodox, traditional Christianity, according to which God is omnipotent, loving, and so forth, and has created the universe. I do not therefore spend much time in defending Christian doctrines, but attempt to show (among other things) that the theory is compatible with them. Occasionally, as in the case of the doctrine of divine omnipotence, for example, I argue for them; but for the most part, except in so far as the tenability of those doctrines relates directly to attacks upon divine command morality, I assume them as given.

I assume too that morality is objective; and apart from a few remarks in the main body of the book I shall not defend that assumption. The Christian belief in the objectivity of morality is so deeply embedded in the dogmas and creeds of the Christian religion that it would be impossible to assume the latter, in its traditional form, without also assuming the former.

Underlying some of my arguments there is, too, the conviction that rationalist accounts of morality are inadequate. Kantian arguments, like those of more recent writers such as Gewirth,[1] as well as older defences of the Golden Rule, tend to rely upon some notion of the equality of persons: what is important for their positions is the universalizability of moral precepts. But I doubt that rational reflection gives us any reason for treating others as our equals. It seems to me that, while it is indeed rational for a man to attempt to further his own interests, he is not similarly placed with regard to furthering the interests of others beyond what is necessary for his own benefit. I do not satisfy my interests simply because there is some interest that requires satisfying, but because (and this distinction is important for my later argument) it is my interest that I want to satisfy. I do not satisfy it because it is the interest of a rational being, but again, because it is mine. From an empirical point of view I see no reason to treat everyone as my equal in the sense required, in cases where self interest dictates that I should do otherwise. In my view, genuine altruism and true personal equality are not concepts that are defensible in the terms of rationalist morality, but require religious support.[2] These points are made, however, only to indicate something of the context of my arguments; as with a number of further assumptions outlined below, a detailed defence is beyond the scope of this work.

Limits of the argument

The subject borders on a very wide range of topics in the philosophy of religion and moral philosophy, and in other areas (for example: divine omnipotence, free will, moral autonomy, moral motivation, necessary truth); any one of these could be developed in detail to form a larger work. But an in depth study of such themes as these is beyond the scope of this book, and is in any case not necessary for the rebuttal of what seem to me to be the chief objections to divine command theory. Thus when I consider autonomy, for instance, my intention is not to develop a thorough account of its nature and its role in morality, but to show that the concept of autonomy which is generally used by those who engage in the debate about the morality of obedience to commands is not seriously affected by the theory, and that any problems which arise are due not to the authoritarian nature of divine commands but to the objectivity of morality.

I have little to say about treatments of the subject which mainly consist in the analysis of the meaning and usage of the terms employed in the debate. This is not merely due to personal preference. In my view the actual subject of such treatments, what they are really about, is quite different from the subject which I am concerned with. The analysis of language may reveal the answers to some philosophical problems, but I do not regard it as having any great bearing upon the questions in divine command theory which I address. The theory's problems arise, I would argue, not from mistaken notions about the meaning of words, nor from the inappropriate usage of terms, but from an inadequate assessment of the consequences for the created universe of divine omnipotence and voluntarism, of God's all powerful will. Much of the debate in this area was conducted long before the commencement of the modern analytical tradition, and can be continued in the same way. I see no need to make use of a modern tool if it is largely inappropriate to the task, no real improvement on the old one, and not particularly suited to my method of working. For similar reasons, I do not consider the treatments of the theory (in its many varieties) in modal and deontic logics.[3]

Techniques and terminology

At times my arguments tend towards the discursive rather than towards a point by point, section by section presentation of the matters at issue. This approach is preferred on two grounds. First, it enables me more easily to follow actual arguments offered by opponents of the theory to wherever they lead, while a selection of various theoretically possible positions for separate discussion would make that more difficult. However, this approach is not adopted exclusively, and I depart from it where appropriate. Further, it applies within individual chapters rather than across the work as a whole; and those chapters can each be regarded as addressing more or less distinct problems, in a logical order. Second, the approach I adopt allows a more natural and less forced treatment of the issues, permitting me to develop at greater length those aspects which I consider most important, and to assume, or to introduce with less argument at convenient places, the more minor, supporting premises.

In general I offer argument for my claims rather than relying for support upon the citation of authorities. As a matter of course I do cite authorities where I make use of or discuss their work, or where they are of particular interest and importance, or where their works can profitably be consulted in respect either of those arguments which I touch upon but do not develop or of those positions which form the assumed context of the work. But the book is not intended to provide an encyclopaedic coverage of every instance of the discussion of divine command theory; it is a defence of a particular position, in which argument is often more suitable than the use of supporting authorities.

I usually make no distinction between the terms 'good' and 'right', or 'bad' and 'wrong', or between 'moral' and 'ethical'. I am aware that those terms have been used with important differences in what they signify; but for my purposes nothing of any consequence turns on the differences and I prefer to follow common usage, and the usage of most of the writers whom I consider, in using them interchangeably. Similarly, except when my argument requires otherwise, I write of 'actions' and 'things' without intending anything of moment to depend on distinguishing them: a 'good action', a 'right action', a 'good thing', a 'right thing' - such terms are often interchangeable, and I make clear those places where they are not.

When I discuss 'the tradition' in Christianity I do not, I believe, make any controversial assumptions. The tradition of Christianity is diverse; but what I often have in mind is the Catholic tradition (which is itself to some degree diverse) because that is large, long standing, and happens to be the one that I am most familiar with, and least ignorant of. It is also, perhaps, more closely associated with opposition to divine command theory than are other branches of Christianity, particularly in relation to natural law morality, and hence provides much material for discussion. But again, there is nothing of any moment in this usage. The aspects of the tradition that I discuss are generally what most educated Christians would accept as forming part of their faith, and I see no sectarian differences affecting the substance of what I have to say.[4] I do occasionally touch upon areas where there are very important sectarian differences - the area of free will is an example - but I make no essential use of arguments which rely on those differences.

Apart from a few instances in which I mention other translations of the Bible, all references to scripture are to the Authorized Version.

Notes

1   Gewirth (1978), *Reason and Morality*, University of Chicago Press: Chicago.
2   Cf. Gascoigne (1985), 'God and Objective Moral Values', *Religious Studies* 21, pp. 531-49, where he notes that accounts which make reason and prudence the basis of morality presuppose a picture of personal equality which reason simply does not supply.
3   For examples of such treatments of the subject see Quinn (1978), *Divine Commands and Moral Requirements*, Clarendon Press: Oxford. See also the two articles by Adams (1987), 'A Modified Divine Command Theory of Ethical Wrongness' (which I do discuss later) and 'Divine Command

Metaethics Modified Again', in his book *The Virtue of Faith*, Oxford University Press: Oxford.

4   That the traditional core of belief was not always what it is now is not my concern, and is in any event controversial. Murray argues, for example, that the concept of omnipotence according to which God can do everything is a post-Augustinian notion, and that the early Christians took it to mean only that God *does* everything - all creation is dependent upon Him. See Murray (1964), *The Problem of God*, Yale University Press: New Haven, pp. 34-5. His view is not easily reconciled with the many scriptural references to God's power (for example, Job 42:2; Mark 10:27).

2 Morality and religion

Introduction

There is an argument against religious morality in general which is meant to show that a straightforward logical error is involved in the derivation of basic moral precepts from religious premises, and that a correct analysis of the matter would show that religious moral precepts would, logically, have to depend upon a prior, non religious awareness of the nature of right and wrong before they could be accepted. If successful, this argument would apply with particular force to divine command theory, which, among various possible religion based moral systems, most emphasizes the complete dependence of morality upon religion. According to the argument, one could not accept that a religion's moral precepts were to be obeyed unless one already knew that what they commanded was good. In following authority in moral matters, if one does not compare the character or nature of that authority (whether it be God, the church, a religious leader, or scripture, or whatever) with a prior concept of right and wrong which is possessed independently of religion then one can not know whether it is itself good or bad; therefore one can not know whether it is to be obeyed, whether what is commanded is right rather than wrong. If one does obey moral precepts which one has not confirmed by reference to one's prior moral knowledge then one acts immorally, or runs the risk of acting immorally, or at any rate acts non morally. Moral activity and awareness are therefore logically prior to religion: the latter must be based on the former, rather than the other way around.

There are several ways of arguing this case; those ways which depend on showing that obedience to authority constitutes an abandonment of the personal moral autonomy that is necessary for truly moral action will be discussed in greater detail later, along with the question of what sort of motivation a moral agent must have. Here I am more concerned with what has been called the autonomy of the moral standard as distinct from that of the moral agent, the idea that morality must be free standing, as it were, and wholly independent of religion, because of the way we necessarily perceive the goodness or rightness of things.[1]

I propose to show that the objection just outlined is one which divine command theory can answer. This can be done in three ways. First, the point can be admitted in part, but in such a way that the role in morality of divine commands is preserved while simultaneously allowing that man requires (and in fact has) an elementary moral awareness which is independent of his knowledge of divine commands (but not independent of God). Second, the main thrust of the objection can be denied outright, and it can be argued instead that we can have direct awareness of moral qualities and obligations without having any prior moral knowledge of the sort that is taken to be necessary by divine command theory's opponents, and which is incompatible with that theory. Third, a different approach can be made which elevates religious morality above secular morality, or rather, denies that the secular variety is genuinely moral. Here it is admitted that knowledge of objective moral duties is available to all, theist and atheist alike, independently of divine commands; but it is held both that divine commands are constitutive of morality and also that truly moral action occurs only in obedience to those commands. The aim of this chapter is not, then, to offer an account which denies all worth to non religious moral systems; nor is it to insist that religion is, after all, logically prior to morality. Rather, it is primarily to show that this criticism of religious morality is not the decisive argument that its proponents take it to be. It fails, I shall argue, for two related reasons: first, it takes insufficient account of the ways in which knowledge, including moral knowledge, may be acquired and held; and second, it does not take enough regard of the nature of religious faith, and particularly of the attitude which the believer adopts towards God.

For convenience, I shall sometimes refer to the objection which is discussed in this chapter as the 'logic objection'; for although several objections to divine command theory are logical in their nature, that name reflects quite well the origin of the objection in the logical analysis of religious morality. During the course of my argument I shall consider, too, an objection with a similar origin, stemming from the logical analysis of the terms employed in the debate.

Acquiring moral knowledge

Consider these words of Kant's:

> We cannot do morality a worse service than by seeking to derive it from examples. Every example of it presented to me must first be judged by moral principles in order to decide if it is fit to serve as an original example - that is, as a model: it can in no way supply the prime source for the concept of

morality. Even the Holy One of the gospel must first be compared with our ideal of moral perfection before we can recognize him to be such... But where do we get the concept of God as the highest good? Solely from the *Idea* of moral perfection... Imitation has no place in morality, and examples serve us only for encouragement...[2]

O'Donovan, referring to Mitchell's treatment of this argument, suggests that the absurdity of Kant's position can be easily demonstrated:

> The radical conception of autonomy which modern humanism consistently adopts from Kant pretends to spear us on a false dilemma, which is meant to demonstrate the irrelevance of authority (all authority, but especially theological) to moral judgment. Either one has already reached a judgment about right and wrong on one's own, so that recognition of 'the Holy One' is not, in the strong sense, acknowledgment of an *authority* at all, or one has not reached it, so that in accepting his authority one acts on non moral grounds. It is in response to this that Basil Mitchell likes to remind us of the Aristotelian 'reasonable man'. By watching and imitating the reasonable man we learn to be reasonable. He deals with the dilemma about autonomy, then, by drawing our attention... to this entirely familiar feature of our moral experience... If the dilemma were a genuine one, if it were in fact the case that we had to make all the reasonable judgments on our own account before we could recognize the reasonable man, then we could never learn by example. The very idea, indeed, of learning by example would be inherently nonsensical. *Quod est absurdum.* Whatever we are to say about the autonomy of moral judgments must at least allow that we can do what we know that we actually do: recognize the authority of a suitable example and learn from our observation and imitation.[3]

Before looking more closely at Mitchell's case against Kant, it is worth considering one response that has been made to the assertion that arguments like Kant's demonstrate the logical priority of morality to religion. Quinn says that what follows from the need to check divine commands against our moral judgment is that the latter (in so far as it relies upon what we already know) has epistemic, not logical priority.[4] In other words, even though we may need to know what good is before we can know that God is good and that His commands are good (or that they are really His), His command may yet be what determines the goodness of an action. So divine commands (or religion) could be logically prior to morality, while *knowledge* of divine commands, knowledge that any command was really issued by God, was logically dependent on knowledge of moral truths. What Quinn says can be countered, though, by an argument that his point is either correct but irrelevant to the divine command theorist's case, or simply incorrect. If it is correct, it shows that God's will *could* be foundational to morality, but allows that our concrete human morality, our moral reasoning and all discourse about what it is right to do or not to do, can proceed without any reference to God; for we know, we need to know, right from wrong independently of whatever religion may tell us.

But that position, though it is perfectly acceptable to an atheist, an agnostic, a Christian Platonist, a natural law moralist, or indeed any opponent of divine command morality, provided he believes that there is such a thing as morality and that we have moral knowledge, is not one which the divine command theorist will want to accept, since his is a stronger claim than it supports. And applying Ockham's razor, why should anyone posit a divine will upon which to ground his knowledge when it seems clear that his knowledge has no need of it? That God's will *might* be foundational (as it *might* be foundational to all existence other than His own) in the sense allowed matters little if we can manage perfectly well without it. If divine commands are foundational only in this way then they seem to be redundant from the moral point of view, since they bear no weight. The divine command theorist who maintained no more than this could not, presumably, be shown to be wrong; he could not, for example, be proved to be inconsistent or at odds with known facts. But his would be a very weak claim, of no particular moral consequence except perhaps to those who, wavering between a belief in the objectivity of morality and a belief in its subjectivity, yet preferring the former, sought for something on which to ground it.

The criticism of Quinn's claim can be taken further: it can be argued that, in the case of morality, epistemological priority *is* logical priority, since morality is *a matter of knowledge*, at least in part.[5] Without knowledge of good and evil, right and wrong, it would make no sense to talk of morality. If moral action consists in doing good, and if doing good is dependent on knowing what is good, then the possibility of morality is dependent upon knowledge. In that case the distinction made by Quinn would not apply to morality, and his claim would not be correct.

If moral action, to be properly so called, depends on moral knowledge then perhaps the criticism of Kant made by Mitchell does not apply. We copy good people, let us say, but our actions are not properly to be described as morally good until a stage in our development which comes after we have achieved the knowledge of good and evil that gives moral character to them. That seems a reasonable position: moral responsibility presupposes moral ability, and that in turn presupposes moral knowledge. The situation can be compared to one which obtains in law, where children below a certain age are presumed not to have the knowledge required for their ostensibly and outwardly illegal actions to be counted as breaches of the law.[6]

If this account of the role of knowledge is correct then we do not learn morality as we learn the steps of a dance, simply by imitating someone else, but locate those things (that is, outward acts) which we have learned by imitation in the context of our developing rational awareness (which does not consist merely in the imitation of outward acts). Whatever the details of the manner in which we learn morality (or reasonableness, which is only a more general term for the same class of thing), this is a question for developmental psychology or sociology: here it is sufficient to note that Kant's argument does not show what is absurd, that learning by example is an impossibility. But it does suggest that learning by example may be more complex an affair than copying one's teacher.

The recognition of expertise in, say, French or mathematics seems not to be genuine recognition (as distinct from mere acknowledgment, for instance) if we have no knowledge of those subjects. For if we are merely repeating an opinion that we have heard or read (as in, 'Professor Smith is the leading expert on hoddy-doddies, but I have no idea what they might be') then we do not *recognize* expertise.[7] We may take the word of a third party, but not presumably without reason to trust him; and even then we still do not *recognize* the expertise in question. There is at this stage, however, the beginning of an admission that we can reasonably trust, though we do not exactly know, that someone has expert knowledge of a matter which we know nothing about. If that is so then one could argue that in morality as in other areas it is reasonable to accept a moral leader as such on the basis of his widely agreed reputation, or on the testimony of other people whom we believe to be good judges of character, well educated, and so forth. Moral expertise is a concept which is ambiguous: it can be the quality that saints have, or it can be that quite different quality that is possessed by, for example, professors of moral philosophy - that is to say, a deep knowledge of moral systems, moral arguments and so forth. In some contexts that distinction will be an important one. Here, however, it is reasonable to suppose that it is irrelevant: it makes no difference whether what is in question is the goodness of character of the supposed moral leader, rather than his knowledge of moral theory. The point, that we could accept third party testimony on such a question even though moral behaviour, to be truly so called, must (so it is felt) follow from or be accompanied by feelings of conviction (as when it is held that we must believe that we are right in order actually to be right in a moral sense), applies to both cases. Even if morality is a special case, so that our imitation of a moral leader and our obedience to moral precepts issued by him would not of itself constitute moral behaviour, we could still have non moral grounds for reasonably supposing (if 'knowing' is deemed too strong a word) that he was indeed an extremely worthy person, someone to be admired, a good man. That judgment does not have to be a moral judgment (in the sense that it is based on our knowledge of good and evil) in order to be accepted as very probably correct.

In any case, someone who defends the morality of following the example of a moral role model does not have to hold that all moral knowledge is learned by, or somehow arises from, the imitation of the good man. One could reject the claim that moral expertise is recognizable without the necessity for prior moral judgment, but hold that such recognition requires only a very basic moral awareness which is available to a wide range of people, or to all rational beings, and which is not learned, or at any rate not learned in any way which depends on earlier moral knowledge which is anything like propositional in nature.[8] It could be held, for instance, that the requisite moral capacity was innate: it could be recovered by *anamnesis* in the course of growing up, or it could be a function of the physical structure of the brain. Indeed, on some different model of morality from that being defended here, one that was based, for example, on the likelihood of the evolution by natural selection of altruistic behaviour in humans, the ability to recognize a moral leader could simply have been bred into us by the accidents of history. The coherence of such accounts is questionable, of course. But all that is being suggested here is that the way in which we recognize moral goodness need not entail the prior possession of any great degree of moral knowledge, and that perhaps what we require is no more than a basic moral awareness. As Mitchell says, it does not take a saint to recognize a saint.[9]

If we are to present an account of morality which makes it thoroughly religious in nature, we need not hold that every moral principle is known only by revelation: one might hold, for instance, that some such principles were innate but God given, and that others were rationally inferable from revealed premises. It may be true that in order for divine command theory to have any substance it would be necessary for it to show that God's commands were relevant to our moral knowledge; but we need not hold that *no* moral knowledge is possible without knowledge of divine commands: it might be possible to show, for instance, that in their absence we could not ground our moral beliefs acceptably, or could not achieve a comprehensive moral system.[10] Nevertheless, one may still feel that in order to do this it is necessary in turn to show that it must be possible to accept a divine command both as genuinely divine in origin and also as the thing to be obeyed, without relying on prior moral knowledge; and that it is a degree implausible to suggest that *that* acceptance stems in some way from innate knowledge, or from some primitive capacity for identifying moral exemplars. What has to be shown is the reason why we should accept any command either as divine in origin or as binding.

Direct awareness of the good

Still, it is a commonly held position among Christians (including those opposed to divine command theory) that we need the help of revelation in order to know, in anything like completeness, what is to be done and what is to be avoided. Man is at a disadvantage in two respects: his awareness is finite and his nature is corrupt. So there will be things that we just do not know about in the world of objective morals; there may be principles which we have never come across, perhaps, but which God knows, since He is omniscient. And there will be matters about which we can not reach correct conclusions, sharing as we do (since the Fall) a liability to temptation and self delusion and a corrupt faculty for moral decision making.

In respect of our finite knowledge, Swinburne[11] suggests that it is this that gives grounds for obedience to divine commands, in the following way. God is omniscient and therefore always knows what is the right thing for us to do. If He tells us to do something then we can be sure that, even though we do not ourselves see the reasons for it or what makes it right, it is bound to be the right thing to do. We can be mistaken about our duties because we do not have all the facts at our disposal, but that can not be the case where God is concerned, since He knows everything there is to be known. Now that account may be acceptable to traditional theists but it will not stand as a way of grounding divine command theory. If we know that God is good, and will not therefore mislead us, and if it is God's omniscience that enables Him to see duties that we can not see, then we may sensibly and morally obey Him. But the former condition is just what is at issue here, while the latter presupposes a Christian Platonist notion of goodness, or something very like it, which is wholly incompatible with divine voluntarism.[12] For the divine command theorist, God does not apprehend the quality of goodness in an action and then proceed to command us to do it; rather, He commands what He will and causally wills the goodness in whatever is good. What is morally right is simply creaturely obedience.

In respect of our corruption, this is the way that Rachels puts the case and gives his counter argument:

> The following expresses a view which has always had its advocates among theologians: 'Men are sinful; their very consciences are corrupt and unreliable guides. What is taken for conscientiousness among men is nothing more than self-aggrandisement and arrogance. Therefore, we cannot trust our own judgment; we must trust God and do what he wills. Only then can we be assured of doing right.'

To which he responds:

> This view suffers from a fundamental inconsistency. It is said that we cannot know for ourselves what is right and what is wrong; and this is because our judgment is corrupt. But how do we know that our judgment is corrupt? Presumably, in order to know that, we would have to know (a) that some actions are morally required of us, and (b) that our own judgment does not reveal that these actions are required. However, (a) is just the sort of thing we can*not* know, according to this view. Now it may be suggested that while we cannot know (a) by our own judgment, we can know it as a result of God's revelation. But even setting aside the practical difficulties of distinguishing genuine from bogus revelation (a generous concession), there is still this problem: if we learn that God (i.e. some being that we take to be God) requires us to do a certain action, and we conclude on this account that the action is morally right, then we have *still* made at least one moral

judgment of our own, namely that whatever this being requires is morally right. Therefore, it is impossible to maintain the view that we do have some moral knowledge, and that all of it comes from God's revelation.[13]

The relevance of man's supposed corruption is discussed by Nielsen too, and what he says supplies in part an answer to the problem as it is put by Rachels:

> Someone might grant that there is this *logical* independence of morality from religion, but still argue that, given man's corrupt and vicious nature (the sin of the Old Adam), he, as a matter of fact, needs God's help to understand what is good and to know what he ought to do. Man is pervasively sinful and there is and always will be much corruption in the palace of justice. Such a response is confused. With or without a belief in God we can recognize such corruption. In some concrete situations at least, we understand perfectly well what is good or what we ought to do. The 'corruption' religious apologists have noted does not lie here. The corruption comes not in our knowledge but in 'our weakness of will.'[14]

Nielsen is right to draw attention both to our ability to recognize corruption and also to *akrasia*, rather than defective knowledge, as being what underlies that corruption. (He is wrong, though, to suppose that our ability to recognize such corruption without having a belief in God is relevant to the claim that we need God's help to know what we ought to do: God's help could be extended to atheists whether or not they know it. Traditionally, conscience has been regarded as a divinely bestowed aid to all men, regardless of their beliefs.) We can not without vicious circularity suppose that our judgment is wholly unreliable: if theists really did believe what Rachels suggests that they believe then he would be right to argue that their position was incoherent. There may of course be some theists who adopt that untenable position,[15] but the traditional Christian view of the matter has long been that conscience in its most basic form (the basic moral awareness mentioned above) is infallible. Potts, having given an account of the mediaeval distinction between *conscientia* and *synderesis*, observes that 'Aquinas' answer to the question whether *synderesis* can do wrong is... that it cannot.'[16] Broadly speaking, *conscientia* is conscience generally, whereas *synderesis* is conscience in its most basic operation, or as Potts puts it, the spark of conscience rather than conscience proper.[17] According to the Catholic *Catechism*,

> Conscience includes the perception of the principles of morality (synderesis); their application in the given circumstances by practical discernment of reasons and goods; and finally judgement about concrete acts yet to be performed or already performed.[18]

It is in respect of the first aspect, the perception of principles, that infallibility is asserted by the tradition, for the good reason that liability to error here would result in the denial of the very possibility of morality. One can not coherently maintain both that some feature is absolutely essential to moral activity and also that it might actually be dispensable, arguing that our insistence upon its indispensability could be a mistake. But it does not follow that Rachels is correct to hold that we can not claim that all the moral knowledge we have comes from revelation. For though it may be true that, without knowledge of some basic aspect of morality (knowledge that we should have to regard as dependable), we should not be in a position to declare that revealed precepts were either divine in origin or moral in content, further consideration will show that nothing of consequence for divine command theory need follow from that admission.

Two claims are being entertained here: first, that morality is impossible if our conscience can not be relied upon; and second, that revealed morality is impossible without some (possibly minimal) prior moral awareness, some ability to recognize the good. The second claim is simply the scripturist's version of the first. More will be said later of the role of conscience in divine command theory, but what is being suggested now is this: Christian divine command moralists can accept that some faculty for moral discernment is required before it can be known that revealed precepts are divine moral commands, and can equate that faculty with synderesis. Logically, it is quite possible that we should be presented with a command, that we should for example come across one written in scripture, and that having considered it we should conclude that what it prescribes for us is a genuine duty which we would never have known about without scripture to tell us; further, it could carry with it some quality which convinced the theist of its divine origin. It was suggested earlier that an innate capacity for recognizing the divine origin of a command was implausible; but conversely, *if theism is true* then perhaps that suggestion is not implausible at all. And obviously, theists think theism is true. They at least ought to concede at this stage that there is a way for divine command theory to meet the principal logic objection that is raised against it. Atheists, correspondingly, should be prepared to admit that, whether or not theism is true, theists could offer a consistent account (in respect at least of this logic objection) of a moral system which was based upon the command of their God being perceived as such without the necessity of its being held up for their moral judgment and approval. Whether this suggestion actually overcomes the original logic objection, and whether it differs substantially from Swinburne's position mentioned above, are matters which depend on the nature of the *divine* element (rather than the merely *good*) which the basic insight or awareness is supposed to apprehend. The viability of the suggestion will be defended below in the context of further argument about what it is like to believe with religious faith.

Actually, a stronger claim in support of divine command theory can be advanced which dispenses with any need for a basic moral judgment which is independent of God's commands, including even the need for synderesis as the faculty which makes morality possible. All traditional theists will presumably agree that a direct, personal confrontation between a man and his God is a real possibility (while again, atheists who concede that theism is possible will admit that this confrontation is a logical possibility). This is what (one may suppose) happens overtly when Jesus chooses the apostles,[19] and in a somewhat different manner when Saul becomes converted on the road to Damascus.[20] The historical accuracy of the scriptures is not a concern here; what is a concern is the possibility that a man should know his God before he knows the Good. If one takes scripture seriously and at face value, where that is reasonable, then one sees that such a possibility is precisely what is being described as actual in the Gospel narrative, for example. We are not led to believe that Simon and Andrew inquire into Jesus's behaviour and character before they follow Him, or that James and John assess His goodness and, finding Him admirable, decide to accompany Him. The details of the narrative suggest that the point of the account is to indicate quite the opposite, namely that something astonishing occurred: the fishing and the net mending are simply abandoned, immediately, at the call of Christ. Historically, in terms of mankind's moral evolution (if such a process has occurred) the development of religious sense *might* have followed upon the prior acquisition of a sense of moral goodness and worth, but it need not have done so. And in terms of the moral development within the life of an individual, it should be noticed similarly that the fact that any one of us generally does have some knowledge of the good before he acquires any awareness of God does not entail that such a sequence is a necessary one, and is not in dispute. We could live otherwise than we now do; we could live in a condition of amorality or total moral ignorance, and still be the sort of creatures who were liable to conversion, capable of acquiring a religious conviction of the good without any intermediate non religious moral conviction. Or at least, *if* we could live in such a state (for it may be argued that a wholly amoral state would be a practical impossibility) such a conversion could not be dismissed as logically impossible. If there are angels and saints then it is fairly easy to imagine that the consequence of one of their number being thrown together with some rogue whom we should not hesitate to criticize as grossly immoral (or even wholly amoral) should be a dramatic religious conversion. In a circumstance such as this it would not appear to be necessary for a man to have prior knowledge of goodness in order to be impressed by direct acquaintance with it, particularly when, instead of some enormously good *creature* being the one to impress, the impression is made by the Creator incarnate. Again, it should be stressed that it is not to the point whether or not such events occurred; what matters is that they could occur, and therefore goodness could be learned, or recognized, by a direct acquaintance of this sort. Abraham could receive, in some overwhelmingly impressive manner, the divine command to sacrifice his son Isaac.[21] Then (perhaps only then) he could get on with the sacrifice in the sure knowledge that it was both commanded by God and the right thing to do.

Divine command theorists do not usually claim to have received their information in such a dramatic way as it may be supposed that Abraham received his, though they may very well believe that their religious faith in more general terms is vouchsafed to them by a direct relationship with God.[22] To ignore this aspect of religion, to ignore what it is like to have faith, is perhaps what leads the critics of religious morality to suppose that something illogical is going on when the faithful give an account of their moral theory. This point will be taken up in greater detail below; but first, there is a further, less weighty, logic based objection to religious morality which needs to be met if divine command theory is to be put forward as a viable system.

The objection from the meaning of 'good'

This objection is based on the logical analysis of language, and concerns the manner in which supporters of divine command theory account for their usage of moral terms such as the word 'good'. As Phillips outlines the objector's position (not his own),

> for believers, 'good' means 'whatever God wills'. But is it not obvious that [this] cannot be the case? If 'good' means 'whatever God wills', the question 'Is what God wills good?' ought to be redundant. Clearly, the question is perfectly meaningful.[23]

Idziak refers to this objection, and to the usual ways of answering it, as follows:

> the *open question* argument can be used against definitions of moral concepts in terms of divine commands: If, e.g., the term 'good' means 'commanded by God', then the question 'Is what God commands good?' ought to be redundant and senseless; since it is a meaningful question, the proposed definition must be wrong. A related form of the argument consists in pointing out that, if divine command morality as a metaethical thesis were correct, then certain propositions (such as 'God's actions are right') would be tautologous, insignificant, or meaningless, which they are not.[24]

She rightly draws attention to the fact that this objection is much older than the modern analytic tradition[25] and adds that the usual modern reply is to the effect that the terms are not used with their ordinary meanings when they occur in the context of divine command metaethics, but that they then constitute stipulative definitions; while she notes that Paley (who was writing, of course, over one hundred years before the publication of Moore's *Principia Ethica* and was not therefore concerned with that form of the objection which relies on Moore's test[26]) argues that we admit such an objection because we are mistaken about the nature of moral rules, having forgotten or lost sight of their divine origin. Quinn's response to what he terms 'the objection from meaning' is to argue that 'our divine command theories ought not to be construed as expressing truths of meaning'; he too thinks that if such a theory were to be so construed then 'it would be silly to ask whether what is commanded by God is required since the claim that what is commanded by God is required amounts to no more than the assertion that what is commanded by God is commanded by God'.[27]

What is astonishing about the way in which the objection has been advanced in modern times is that it relies upon the apparently uncritical acceptance by the objectors of such a patently false proposition stemming from Moore's work, namely, that if 'X is Y' is a definition (or a truth of meaning) then it is senseless to ask 'Is Y X?'. To be sure, the next step of the argument involves the correct application of *modus tollens* (it is not senseless to ask 'Is Y X?', therefore 'X is Y' is not a definition); but the premise to which it is applied is still false. Consider such questions as these: 'Does a triangle have three sides?'; 'Is a bachelor an unmarried man?'; 'Is *un homme heureux* a fortunate man?'. Each of these questions makes perfect sense; but each would have to be dismissed as senseless if the argument that is the 'objection from meaning' had any validity. And if, as is perhaps the case, the objector's use of the term 'senseless' is really a loose and inaccurate way of saying 'pointless', then it is to be insisted upon that these questions need by no means be pointless, and that circumstances are readily envisaged in which such questions are eminently sensible and rational ones to ask. Coming respectively from a child, a learner of English, and a learner of French; coming from someone who does not possess a full and accurate account of the meaning of the terms in question; coming from one who has not made a complete analysis of the terms; coming from someone who is mistaken about their meaning or who has forgotten it; coming, quite simply, from someone who does not already know the answers: *of course* the questions have point and make sense. Putting the matter bluntly: if the divine command theorist is right in his account then his opponents are wrong, and their position is therefore analogous to that of the questioning child, or learner; it is the position of the ignorant, the mistaken, the forgetful, the confused, and so forth. What it makes sense to ask depends in general on the circumstances of the question, and in particular on the level of knowledge of the questioner. If God's commands really are what make right whatever is right, then 'Is what God commands right?' is a sensible question for some (relatively ignorant) people to ask but not for other (relatively enlightened) people to ask.

Faber[28] takes up the objection that divine command theory makes all moral claims about God into tautologies, and points out that there are clearly instances where the theory does not do this: when we say that God is just, for example, we do not suppose that justice consists in whatever God's actions should be. On the contrary: the claim is that as a matter of fact, God acts towards men in the manner that we call 'just'; He displays a characteristic which has something in common with just men. And in respect of the allegedly tautologous nature of the claim that God is good, Faber notes that the divine command theorist usually adopts a position which is rather different from the one his critics tend to attribute to him: he holds that X is right *because* God wills it, and this is not equivalent to the claim that X is right *if and only if* God wills it.[29] To suppose that the divine command moralist's account of the meaning of 'right' is purely a matter of language is, perhaps, to miss the point of that account. What he may intend primarily to convey is that 'good' means 'commanded by God' in the sense that the ultimate explanation of the term, its correct analysis, is to be made in terms of the divine will. This is the gist of Quinn's response to the objection, mentioned above. However, no such qualification is necessary: the contention that divine command theory makes (some) moral claims about God into tautologies can simply be accepted. No adverse consequences follow for the theory from such an admission. For, as with the question of what it makes sense to ask, the answer to which must be related to the knowledge of the enquirer, so too with the importance of the tautological nature of moral statements about God: tautologies can be informative, even revelatory, depending on the state of knowledge or ignorance of the man who encounters them. If divine commands are the foundation of morality then 'What God wills is right' may indeed be tautologous; but that it is tautologous may not be obvious to someone in an early stage of moral development. The moral *cognoscenti* will discern the tautology, but no one else will. That position is quite consistent with a majority belief that such a claim is *not* tautologous, for most people do not have (so it can be assumed) sufficient knowledge to reach the correct conclusion about the true nature of morality. Whether or not such statements are tautologous is of little consequence, then. Phillips, in giving his own reply to the position he raises concerning the redundancy or senselessness of questioning the goodness of God, writes thus: 'But why should the question be redundant? God's will does not cease to mean what it does simply because it is questioned.'[30] Similarly, neither the content of the divine will as expressed in God's commands, nor the practical consequences of those commands for human action, need be affected one whit by the discovery of the enlightened that, contrary to what was previously thought, the things that people had been saying about God proved to be tautologous. Tautologies are not necessarily (nor, perhaps, usually) empty.

Conclusion

Christians do not stand to God in the same relation as pupils to a moral teacher, or admirers to a moral role model. It is in the nature of the faith that its adherents do not subject the precepts of God to scrutiny. This indeed is the ground of much of the criticism that has been brought against religious morality. But there is a danger of misunderstanding the relation of the Christian to his God, construing it in such a way that the nature of his morality is distorted. In the writings of Saint Paul, or the prayers of Saint Augustine or Saint Anselm, the devotion expressed towards God is total; but it is a very different form of devotion from that which would allow a devotee to say, 'I have judged you to be a good moral leader and will follow you and obey your command whatever it may be, because I trust you always to command rightly'. And it is clearly different from the devotion which permits the violation of conscience: 'I trust you to command rightly and will even do at your behest what I believe to be wrong'. Any divine command moralist who maintained *that* would have his theory properly dismissed as either incoherent or immoral. Abraham does not love God so much that he is prepared to conform to the divine will even when he believes it to be wrong; nor does the divine command prompt any inner struggle or crisis of faith or conscience. The point to be grasped here is not that the text does not warrant either of these conclusions, but that an understanding of what it is to believe in God, to believe in Jehovah of the Jewish and Christian religions, shows that they can not be correct. The adherents of the faith do not, as has just been said, subject the precepts of God to scrutiny. But this is not because they believe that such scrutiny would be disloyal or disrespectful. Scrutiny of divine commands in the sense of examining whether they are morally right is simply pointless, not because of God's omniscience and presumed goodness but because part of what it is to believe in Him, as He is taken to be by the tradition and not simply as one might assent to a philosophical proposition, involves conforming one's will to His will. If one believed that one had received a divine command then *conscience would dictate* that it be obeyed. Someone who follows overwhelming and compelling inner voices which bid him kill his children may be condemned as a psychopath, but he can hardly be condemned on the moral ground that he submitted to the authority of someone else knowing it to be wrong; and an 'inner voice' is often what conscience is described as.

The nature of faith does not preclude the sort of theoretical examination of the morality of divine commands which might be undertaken in an academic context, for example; what it precludes is an examination, for the purpose of discerning whether or not it is right, of what God is known or believed to have commanded. That is precluded not by feelings of deference or respect, nor by a necessary subservience, but by logic, because the conviction that His command is right is included in the faith that the believer has in Him.[31]

> *Our moral life has its source in faith in God* who reveals his love to us. Saint Paul speaks of the 'obedience of faith' as our first obligation. He shows that 'ignorance of God' is the principle and explanation of all moral deviations. Our duty toward God is to believe in him and to bear witness to him[32]

- that is one way of expressing the believer's necessary affirmation of the primacy of faith, the priority of that faith to morality. That priority is an entailment of the manner in which faith is held and is unaffected by the temporal sequences in the development of moral and religious knowledge which may obtain within the life of any one of the faithful. In view of this, one can reverse the objection discussed above and argue that, to the true believer, it makes *no sense whatever* to question the goodness of God's commands.

The concept of traditional Christianity is one that admits of a range of positions, and the traditional believer may dispute the account given here of the nature and consequences of faith. But if faith really is as I have just suggested then it can safely be supposed that God can bestow the gift of it upon a complete moral ignoramus: one *could* have knowledge of divine commands before being able to tell the difference between right and wrong. The first of the above three responses to the logic objection to divine command morality is therefore a viable possibility. The situation envisaged differs from one in which a modicum of moral knowledge is supplemented by divine commands, which would then, so it is argued, be assessed for moral content on the basis of what was already known, and which could not therefore be foundational to morality. It differs too from the position put forward by Swinburne which also presupposes some moral knowledge which is prior to knowledge of God. For what this first response posits is a basic prior awareness of divinity, rather than of moral truths. It includes, to be sure, a moral component, but not in any way which makes religion logically dependent on morality. One may think of it as the spark of faith rather than the spark of conscience; and the faith of which it is a spark could be as suggested above, in which case it would encompass, rather than depend on, morality.

This conception of faith is relevant too to the second response to the logic objection, according to which direct awareness of God removes the need for prior moral knowledge: one accepts His commands because one accepts Him, so to speak. On this account, what is produced in a creature as a result of a direct confrontation with His creator is faith of a sort that includes the certainty of the goodness of the Creator. Of course, an atheist may deny the very possibility (in terms, that is, of physical possibility) of such an encounter, though perhaps he will not want to deny the *logical* possibility that it should occur. But that is of less relevance to the account than what seems to be a more defensible claim, namely that such meetings just do not happen in the lives of most adherents of religious morality. An objector may hold, that is to say, that the moral position of most religious moralists, including most divine command moralists, is illogical. He may grant that there are or could be a few rare and fortunate people whose direct acquaintance with God exempts their moral stance from this criticism, but point out that he is criticizing not these merely possible individuals but his real religious opponents who make no claim to the possession of such direct knowledge. That my moral code *could* depend on the will of God is no defence against the objection that its illogicality lies in its not in fact depending on that will: in order to make that defence what needs to be shown is that it is not illogical as it actually stands. For the divine command theorist, this involves a demonstration of how his acceptance of the goodness of God's commands is to be justified without relying either on prior moral knowledge or on experiences of an Abrahamic or Pauline nature.

The third response available to the logic objection will meet this concern and will show, again relying on the conception of faith outlined above, what the divine command theorist may take to be the actual case rather than a bare logical possibility. It was noted above that the temporal priority of moral to religious knowledge - a sequence which is quite possible, and even probable - did not preclude the possibility of the logical priority of religious knowledge. Consider then one possible progression in the moral development of a person: suppose that he starts his adult life with a broadly utilitarian moral outlook acquired while maturing but for the most part unexamined. He then becomes a Christian, with moral reasoning and motives playing some part in his conversion, and modifies his moral position in the light of the religious doctrines to which he now assents, moving towards natural law morality, for example. Finally his deeper examination both of the nature of morality and of the nature of the God he has come to believe in leads him to espouse divine voluntarism and a moral system which is based upon the commands of God. In this man we should have an example of someone whose belief in God depended in part upon his prior moral convictions yet who maintained that morality was entirely dependent upon divine commands. Why should there be any inconsistency in this position? A sound argument may produce a conclusion which shows that one of the premises used to arrive at that conclusion was unjustified (though true). An acceptance of secular morality may be the starting point in that journey towards a knowledge of God which shows that secular morality can not be sustained without the support of further, religious premises. The conclusion of a sound argument may not (normally[33]) show that one of its premises was *false*. Likewise, a belief in God which relies on a prior, secular conception of morality can not rationally coexist with the supposition that secular morality is false. Caution is needed at this point, though, since the claim that secular morality is false is ambiguous. One can rely on its precepts while rejecting its ultimate secular grounding and justification as false; and in *that* sense one can depend on it while believing it to be false. But if one relies on its precepts while at the same time believing them to be untrue then one's position has become incoherent.

The divine command moralist will accept the truth of many, perhaps most of the precepts of secular morality, though he will want to add a few more of his own, and his justification of the whole set of moral precepts will be different from that of his secular counterpart. He does not suppose that the truth value of propositions such as 'It is wrong to tell lies or to steal' varies with the speaker, being false for secular utilitarians but true for Ockhamists.

It is nevertheless possible to maintain an important distinction between the actions of the adherents of secular and religious moral systems even when they obey the same precepts and perform what are to all appearances actions of the same sort. A course of action may be the morally correct one, objectively speaking, while undertaken in ignorance of proper moral motivation, or for illicit gain, or for some ignoble end, say. In this case the religious moralist can argue that someone who does what is objectively right does not do what is right subjectively speaking. From this point of view his behaviour lacks some element (here, the intention to obey God) which is necessary for genuine moral action. On an account of this sort it is possible to say that the convert envisaged above acted *correctly* when, before conversion, he followed his conscience and his utilitarian code (to the extent that these coincided with actions that religious morality would prescribe); but he did not perform *morally right* actions.[34] After his conversion he came to understand that acts had to accord with human nature in order to be right; and later still, he realized that what constituted human nature was itself a matter which was ordained by divine will and command. With hindsight he could see that many of his previous actions were correct, but that his actions only became morally right in the context of what he had learned of the complete dependence of all creation upon God both for its existence and for its attributes.[35] This theocentric understanding of the universe relies upon an earlier understanding of right and wrong, and he would not have come to believe in a God who had the nature of the Lord of the Flies; but with new insight he could now accept that what seemed unalterably right or wrong was in fact contingent upon the divine will.

What this man acquires during the process of religious conversion (in addition to a new outlook) is faith in God. What is more, he represents more convincingly than the subject of dramatic divine encounters the ordinary believer who feels some form of direct connection to God and who possesses all the beliefs necessary for a rationally defensible acceptance of divine voluntarism.

It would be possible then to come to believe that morality is dependent on God's command even though one did not come to know of God's command without the use of some prior moral knowledge. And those occasions when the theory may differ in content, as well as in the manner of its justification, from secular moral theory, may yet prove to be crucial. If the foregoing remarks about faith and the religious outlook are accepted, then it will be seen that, for the believer, divine command morality may yield precepts which could not possibly be rationally inferred (though their acceptance would be rational) but which may be of the utmost importance.[36]

Notes

1   To some extent these arguments overlap. The distinction is not a sharp one, but the structure of my argument makes it more convenient to postpone some discussion until later. Cf. Woods (1966), *A Defence of Theological Ethics*, Cambridge University Press: Cambridge, p. 8.

2   From Kant's *Groundwork of the Metaphysic of Morals*. Here I quote from the translation in Paton (1987), *The Moral Law*, Hutchinson: London, p. 73.

3   O'Donovan (1987), 'The Reasonable Man: An Appreciation', in Abraham and Holtzer, *The Rationality of Religious Belief*, Oxford. For Basil Mitchell's argument see his (1980), *Morality: Religious and Secular*, Oxford University Press: Oxford, particularly p. 148.

4   Quinn (1978), *Divine Commands and Moral Requirements*, Clarendon Press: Oxford, p. 9. The actual argument he is discussing is in Rachels (1971), 'God and Human Attitudes', *Religious Studies* 7, pp. 325-37.

5   Alternatively, one could make use of the distinction that is sometimes made between 'good' and 'right', and show that morality relied on the latter: an action could be good in some unknowable, metaphysical sense by being commanded by God, but would only be morally right when done in the light of moral knowledge.

6   A similar position obtains in church law, according to which sin can not be attributed to children before they have reached the 'age of reason' at which they are able to acquire genuine moral knowledge. Cf. also Aristotle, *Eudemian Ethics* III, 1228b, where he distinguishes between what is good or pleasant absolutely, and what is so to e.g. 'children qua children'.

7   The same point can be made by using an unknown foreign term, when the situation perhaps becomes more clear: 'He is an expert on *feòir*'. Anyone who uttered that statement, and had no knowledge of Gaelic whatever, would literally not know what he was talking about.

8   Mitchell, op. cit., p. 147, argues that all that is needed is some incipient awareness of goodness, rather than a full understanding of it.

9   Mitchell, op. cit., ibid.

10   See for instance Garnett (1955), *Religion and the Moral Life*, New York, p. 13: 'the claim to revelation in matters of morals is understood by the traditionalist (if he represents a clearly thought out tradition) as either reinforcing or specifically pointing out a duty which is knowable independently of revelation, *or as adding to the general moral law some special duty, depending upon man's religious relationships*'; emphasis mine.

11   Swinburne (1977), *The Coherence of Theism*, Oxford University Press: Oxford. See particularly chapter 11, 'Perfectly good and a source of moral

obligation', pp. 179-209. See too Swinburne (1974), 'Duty and the Will of God', *Canadian Journal of Philosophy* IV, 2, pp. 213-27. The argument of Swinburne's which I discuss here is discussed later in more depth.

12 I discuss Christian Platonism, together with the concept of necessary moral truth (upon which Swinburne relies) in detail later.
13 Rachels, op. cit.
14 Nielsen (1985), *Philosophy and Atheism*, New York, p. 175.
15 Cf. the account in Mouw (1990), *The God Who Commands*, p. 68.
16 Potts (1980), *Conscience in Medieval Philosophy*, Cambridge University Press: Cambridge, p. 48. He suggests (p. 64) that the motivation of those who insisted on the infallibility of *synderesis* was theological, deriving from Romans 2:15-16, where St. Paul's assertion that the law is written on men's hearts is taken to mean that there is an aspect of conscience which is innate and unmistakable. However, his account of Aquinas's reasoning, where the motivation is a logical one, could equally apply to that of anyone else, in agreement with what I say concerning the coherence of doubting the reliability of one's own judgment. Aquinas's reason is 'that the whole edifice of knowledge, whether theoretical or practical, rests upon basic principles, so that, if we could be wrong about these, nothing would be certain' (p. 48).
17 Ibid., p. 10.
18 *Catechism of the Catholic Church* (1994), Vatican, section 1780, p. 396.
19 Matthew 3:18-22.
20 Acts 9:3-18.
21 Genesis 22:2.
22 We are told (Genesis 22:1-2) that God 'put Abraham to the test' (New World Translation) and what He is supposed to have said, but not the manner of the telling or the circumstances surrounding it. Suitably impressive circumstances are easily and reasonably imaginable, however.
23 Phillips (1966), 'God and Ought', in Ramsey (ed.) *Christian Ethics and Contemporary Philosophy*, London, p. 133. This objection is made in another article in this collection: de Graaff (in 'God and Morality', p. 33) says that 'good' can not mean 'commanded by God' because it makes sense to ask whether what God commands is really good.
24 Idziak (1979), *Divine Command Morality: Historical and Contemporary Readings*, Edwin Mellen Press: New York, p. 19.
25 Op. cit., p. 20. She cites eighteenth century works by Francis Hutcheson, Richard Price and William Paley.
26 The 'open question argument' is due to Moore (1903), *Principia Ethica*, Cambridge University Press: Cambridge. William Paley's arguments are to be found in his (1785), *The Principles of Moral and Political Philosophy*, London.

27 Op. cit., pp. 39-41.
28 Faber (1985), 'The Euthyphro Objection to Divine Normative Theories: A Response', *Religious Studies* 21, pp. 559-72.
29 In this connection see Wierenga (1989), *The Nature of God*, Cornell University Press; and also Wierenga (1983), 'A Defensible Divine Command Theory', *Nous* 17, pp. 387-407.
30 Op. cit., p. 137.
31 My point is not that of Rachels, op. cit., who argues that recognition of God includes a commitment to *obedience*, but that such recognition includes a commitment to assenting to His *goodness*, and that this is not a consequence of creaturely subservience.
32 *Catechism of the Catholic Church* (1994), Vatican, section 2087, p. 454; emphasis mine.
33 I ignore here the *consequentia mirabilis*, where a conclusion -p is inferred from a premise p; such an argument may be sound in the sense of being safe and dependable, even if not formally sound in the logicians' sense; as the name implies, that case is, precisely, not normal. For in the circumstances which I describe, it is *what is true* in secular morality which underpins subsequent beliefs. Nor do I mean to deny that later (true) beliefs could somehow have been brought about by earlier (false) beliefs which could then be discarded. But those earlier beliefs can not be discarded while they continue to act as supports, in the sense intended here, for the later ones.
34 Similarly, a divine command moralist may deny that an atheist, for instance, *truly knows* that e.g. murder is wrong - he could say, taking the definition of knowledge as justified, true belief, that his opponent's belief that murder is wrong is not adequately justified.
35 Cf. Simon (1967), *The Tradition of Natural Law*, New York, p. 62: 'Acquaintance with natural law, being a way to God, would be logically antecedent to the knowledge of God's existence. But from this logical priority in the order of discovery it does not follow that the understanding of natural law can be logically preserved in case of failure to recognize in God the ultimate foundation of all laws.' A related point, that the epistemological problem of determining God's existence is not relevant to the ontological question whether moral rightness might be dependent on divine command, is made by Oakes (1972), 'Reply to Professor Rachels', *Religious Studies* 8, pp. 165-67.
36 'Being known only by divine revelation does not entail being logically dependent on theology' according to Frankena. See his article (1981), 'Is Morality Logically Dependent on Religion?', in Helm, *Divine Commands and Morality*, Oxford University Press: Oxford, p. 26. But it does entail just that - either if the information which God reveals is not to be based

on something resembling the knowledge He has according to a Christian Platonist account (an account which I discuss and reject later), or if the essential role of knowledge in morality is as indicated in the above arguments.

3 Autonomy, obedience and power

Introduction

In the previous chapter it was argued that one need not have any prior moral awareness in order to see that a divine command was rightly to be obeyed, and that the nature of faith offered a way out of the supposed logical impasse presented by an account which gave priority to religion over morality. Here I propose a different defence of the position in the face of a related objection, that without such prior knowledge one somehow abandons one's responsibility in the commitment one gives to obey the commands of another being; one does not act with the personal moral autonomy which is necessary for genuinely moral action to occur. What I shall suggest is that the nature of divine omnipotence, far from being an unworthy ground for creaturely devotion, actually guarantees that what it ordains is good. In brief, the claim put forward in the following defence of the theory amounts to this: divine omnipotence is not incoherent, and it entails divine goodness; it is precisely because He is omnipotent that the commitment to obey God does not constitute an abandonment of moral autonomy on a creature's part; and this is so regardless of the presence in the believer of the 'spark of faith' discussed earlier.

Omnipotent God

The Catholic *Catechism* contains a statement of the traditional Christian belief in the omnipotence of God which indicates that doctrine's centrality and its strength:

> Of all the divine attributes, only God's omnipotence is named in the Creed: to confess this power has great bearing on our lives. We believe that his might is *universal*, for God who created everything also rules everything and can do everything... The Holy Scriptures repeatedly confess the *universal* power of God... If God is almighty 'in heaven and on earth' it is because he made them. Nothing is impossible with God, who disposes his works according to his will. He is the Lord of the Universe, whose order he established and which remains wholly subject to him and at his disposal.[1]

The tradition is of course diverse, and though all branches of it might accept this account, not all would allow its interpretation to yield the sort of claims made by, for example, William of Ockham.[2] The theory of divine command morality which is to be defended here is in essence the same as his, and it relies heavily upon an Ockhamist conception of the power of God.

For Ockham, as Copleston explains, 'God can do anything or order anything'; and what is right (or wrong) is so for no other reason than that God has commanded (or forbidden) it; and He did not have to command (or forbid) it.

> His thesis was that such acts [as adultery, fornication, theft, hatred of God etc.] are wrong because God has forbidden them... He made use of the distinction between the absolute power (*potentia absoluta*) of God, by which God could order the opposite of the acts which He has, as a matter of fact, forbidden, and the *potentia ordinata* of God, whereby God has actually established a definite moral code. But he explained the distinction in such a way as to make it clear not only that God could have established another moral order but that He could at any time order what He has actually forbidden. There is no sense, then, in seeking for any more ultimate reason of the moral law than the divine *fiat*. Obligation arises through the encounter of a created free will with an external precept. In God's case there can be no question of an external precept. Therefore God is not obliged to order any kind of act rather than its opposite. That He has ordered this and forbidden that is explicable in terms of the divine free choice; and this is a sufficient reason.[3]

God's omnipotence is, then, the highest degree of power, power to do anything whatever, *potentia absoluta* in the sense just given. This is not to be compromised: it is largely out of the conviction that alternative accounts of morality (such as are offered by Christian Platonists, or Catholic natural law moralists, for instance) fail to do justice to the power of God that divine command theory is proposed in the first place. Yet there are two ways in which God's omnipotence is sometimes said to be restricted. First, He is often said to be in some manner constrained by His own nature. Thus the *Catechism* account continues:

> God's almighty power is in no way arbitrary: 'In God, power, essence, will, intellect, wisdom, and justice are all identical. Nothing can therefore be in God's power which could not be in his just will or his wise intellect.'[4]

And Johnson, writing of the God of the Jewish tradition, says 'Nor was he all-powerful since, as judge, he was bound by his own law';[5] that comment might equally be applied to the God of the Christian tradition.

The question whether it makes sense to consider God as constrained in any way by aspects of His own nature such as His justice, His goodness and so forth, will be considered in later chapters. Here the primary concern is with a second supposed restriction on His power: He is generally held to be bound by the laws of logic. I take it to be obvious, however, that the notion of 'restricted omnipotence' is incoherent: if God's power is in any way restricted then He is *not* omnipotent. (This is not to deny that God restricts His actions. That He could perform acts X, Y and Z, but chooses to perform X and Y only is not a limitation of His power to perform Z.) But to hold that God is genuinely omnipotent is not to place His actions outside the laws of logic: God must, it is true, conform His actions to the 'restrictions' of logic; but that is not really any constraint at all. From the fact that God can not breach the law of non contradiction, can not simultaneously (ignoring, here, considerations of eternity and timelessness[6]) make true both a proposition p and its contradictory -p, can not create the world in which a situation S obtains alongside its contradictory -S, it does not follow that there is something which God can not do. That God can not make a square circle, or any other logically impossible entity, is a consequence of there being no such thing to create: a logical impossibility is not truly a thing at all, and the inability to create one can not therefore be sensibly supposed to be a genuine restriction upon God.

Aquinas says that 'nothing which implies contradiction falls under the omnipotence of God';[7] and Lewis expands upon this: 'His omnipotence includes power to do all that is intrinsically possible, not to do the intrinsically impossible. You may attribute miracles to Him, but not nonsense'.[8]

It may be a corollary of this argument, depending upon the view one takes about the relation between God's will and His commands, that God can not issue contradictory commands. Quinn supposes that there is no contradiction in assuming that He can.[9] However, he also holds that 'it is at the deepest level God's will, and not his commands, which merely express his will, that determines the deontological status of actions'.[10] But if a divine command is the true expression of God's will then He can not issue a command of the form 'p and -p' because He can not will it, there being no 'it', no circumstance corresponding to a logical contradiction, for Him to will. One can argue that a command which is not intended to be obeyed is not truly a command; then if God seems to issue contradictory commands they can not be genuine commands, for He can not intend that they be obeyed: that would be tantamount to willing a contradiction. It follows too that God can not command what is physically impossible. For, as far as traditional theism is concerned, one's physical powers are creations of God's will: I am what I am because He wills it so.[11] Then if God were to command me to do what is physically impossible He would have to will both my physical limitations and, what is contradictory, my ability to surpass those limitations. If He commanded me to fly then He would have to will (given that I can not do it) that I should both be able and unable to do so. Of course, God might will a change in my nature to enable me to fly, but in that case I should not be commanded to do what is physically impossible.

So, there may be no contradiction in assuming that God might tell us both to observe and not to observe the Sabbath, say; but such a divine utterance would have to be viewed as a puzzle, perhaps, or at any rate as something not to be taken literally. It could not be taken as a genuine command. If it is supposed that human perfection is a physical impossibility, then the Gospel instruction to be perfect[12] has to be interpreted along the lines of a command to attempt or aim at perfection.

This conception of unrestricted power as being what underlies the moral order gives rise to two quite different attacks upon the theory of divine command morality. First, it may be held that the concept of omnipotence which the theory makes use of is incoherent. Alternatively, it is often supposed that the obedience which must be given to God amounts, on the divine command account, to mere prudence, or else entails an unjustifiable equation of might with right, of power with goodness. And, it is held, such obedience requires an abandonment of the personal moral autonomy which is necessary for genuine moral action to take place.[13]

The first objection can be dealt with quite briefly. It has been argued that the concept of omnipotence gives rise to irresolvable paradoxes.[14] Can God create a stone that is too heavy for Him to lift? Can He (extending omnipotence to omniscience - extending 'power' to 'power to know') create a person with a secret that no one else, Himself included, knows? Such questions allegedly lead to the denial of divine omnipotence whether they are answered in the affirmative or the negative.

There is a danger that an inadequate account of omnipotence will result in the proposal of a solution to these questions which involves either an infinite regress or vicious circularity. Van den Brink, having offered a similar argument to that above in justification of the traditional view that omnipotence means power to do anything that is logically possible, writes:

> Once we have decided that omnipotence should only quantify over states of affairs which it is logically possible to actualize, (or over actions which it is logically possible to perform), many possible solutions to further problems are predetermined. For example, the paradoxes of omnipotence can now be dealt with by claiming that actions such as creating an object which its maker cannot destroy are logically impossible for an omnipotent agent to

perform, and that hence its inability to perform them does not entail that the agent is not omnipotent.[15]

But one can not usefully define an omnipotent being as one able to perform any action logically available to an omnipotent being: on that account, omnipotence is the power to do anything provided it is compatible with omnipotence. That may be an accurate statement but it gives no content to omnipotence, and does not meet the problems raised by the paradoxes. Similarly, one can not usefully define God's power by reference to other attributes He may have, if the definitions of those other attributes make reference to His power: to say that He can not do things that are incompatible with His omniscience and that He can not know things that are incompatible with His omnipotence will leave one quite unable to break out of a circle of definitions.

It is possible, though, to combine an insistence that whatever He is credited with being able to do should be a logical possibility, with an intuitive understanding of the difference between a capacity to do something, a capability, and an incapacity, an inability to do something. That a very strong man could not *not* lift a hundredweight sack of coal, that is, that he could fail to lift it if he tried, would not normally be taken to imply any lack of power on his part. That a very learned man did not know how it felt not to know some proposition which was basic to his profession would not normally be considered a defect in his knowledge. One may say that it is intuitively obvious that an omnipotent being can create stones of every conceivable weight, and can, ignoring problems of incorporeality, lift every conceivable stone. That the distinction between an ability and the lack of an ability is sometimes an intuitive one which resists explanation (the ability to solve a problem counts as just that - an ability; but the 'ability' to be baffled by a problem does not count as an ability at all) does not entail that it is not a coherent distinction. Presumably, when we term something an ability rather than an inability, this relates to what it is in a wider context that we wish to do. In the context of morality, for example, it might be said that an inability to harm someone or to tell lies is actually a strength: 'he couldn't hurt a fly' can be taken as an indication of virtuous character rather than of weakness. In fact, it is not strictly necessary that a definition of what it is to be omnipotent should specify what is to count as an ability and what is to count as an inability. If the realization of every conceivable state of affairs, or every possible action, is taken in total to form a (possibly infinitely large) set, such that the whole set includes both actions or states of affairs and their contradictories, then an omnipotent being can perform or realize together half of the set, namely that subset which does not contain both an action or state of affairs and its contradictory. God can therefore do anything which does not entail a contradiction: He can, one may assume, bring it about that an event should occur on a certain date at a certain place, or He can bring it about that it should not, but He can not do both. An understanding by us of what particular actions He can or can not perform will require an investigation into whether the consequences of any possible action entail a contradiction, and may therefore be something which is quite beyond our reach; but the coherence of the concept of omnipotence is not undermined by our human limitations.

There is, in any case, a further, decisive way of responding to the questions which supposedly generate paradoxes. Can God make a stone which He can not lift? Yes: if He is omnipotent then of course He can. The question is whether God can do something which results in His ceasing to be omnipotent. It is, in effect, whether God can by act of will cease to be omnipotent. That He can does not in any way suggest either that the concept of omnipotence is incoherent or that He is not after all omnipotent. The correct response to the objection that God would not, after the act, be omnipotent is to deny that such a consequence is in any way objectionable. Naturally, if God were to act so as to stop being omnipotent then He would no longer be omnipotent. There is nothing paradoxical about that. This line of attack on the position of the divine command theorist who wishes to make use of the concept of omnipotence can be successfully resisted then.

Autonomy and obedience

Let us take it both that the necessity to act in accordance with logic is no constraint upon God's omnipotence and also that there is nothing incoherent about the concept of omnipotence. We are left with God's unfettered word as the basis of morality: to do what is morally right is just to obey Almighty God who commands as He will. Now consider some of the objections that have been advanced against this position, on grounds connected with personal moral autonomy.

Nielsen argues that 'if we do what we do simply because it has been authorized, we cannot be reasoning and acting as moral agents; for to respond as a moral agent, one's moral principle must be something which is subscribed to by one's own deliberate commitment, and it must be something for which one is prepared to give reasons'.[16] MacNamara makes a similar point:

> If then morality involves the notions of responsibility, of autonomy, if it is about seeing as much as doing, if it is about the recognition of a claim, there are important pointers for what might be called church morality. Morality cannot be about obedience. The claim of morality is the claim of the truth and a true moral response is some recognition of that claim.[17]

Daly gives further content to the objection. After giving Kant's view, that 'to be religious is to view our duties as divine commands', he says that some religious moralists

> have, as it were, reversed the order of Kant's dictum... Instead, they have in effect acted according to some such dictum as: 'To be moral is to view divine

commands as our duty'... Morality which does not arise out of inner conviction is scarcely more than the prudent conventions of the parade-ground, where soldiers obey their superior officers for pragmatic reasons.[18]

A different aspect of the objection is voiced by Nowell-Smith:

> There is nothing in the idea of an omnipotent, omniscient creator which, by itself, entails his goodness or his right to command, unless we are prepared to assent to Hobbes' phrase, 'God, who by right, that is by irresistible power, commandeth all things.' Unless we accept Hobbes' consistent but repugnant equation of God's right with his might, we must be persuaded independently of his goodness before we admit his right to command.[19]

An argument against the last point of Nowell-Smith's has already been given earlier. Here the primary concern is the relation of God's power to His goodness. Meynell recognizes the importance of an adequate account which connects might and right, remarking upon the absence of any proof that the former entails the latter.[20] And Goldstick notes that any such entailment would preclude the existence of an omnipotent demon.[21] He considers, however, that an almighty demon could exist, adding that the obedience given by a creaturely moral agent, where omnipotence is the ground of that obedience, is unworthy and inconsistent with moral autonomy.

Consider next two proposed answers to the question why one should obey God's commands, the first offered by Geach, and the second by Swinburne. According to Geach, it would be insane to disobey an all powerful deity. The traditional theist can accept this, for he believes that disobedience will have disastrous consequences; though it should be noted that such consequences are not necessary - an omnipotent deity might be prepared to tolerate the disobedience of its creatures. However, assuming a Christian context, the eternal punishment which could be the price to be paid for disobedience will certainly outweigh any short term advantage that a moral agent gains by ignoring divine commands. Geach defends his position, against the objection that obedience given to Almighty God solely because He is Almighty amounts to mere power worship, in the following way:

> But since this is worship of the Supreme Power, it is as such wholly different from, and does not carry with it, a cringing attitude towards earthly powers. An earthly potentate does not compete with God, even unsuccessfully: he may threaten all manner of afflictions, but only from God's hands can any affliction actually come upon us. If we fully realize this, we shall have such fear of God as destroys all earthly fear.[22]

So obedience to God is indeed obedience to power, but it is more noble and rational than obedience to mere earthly power.

Swinburne, in an argument touched upon earlier, takes a different line: it is God's omniscience that provides us with a reason to obey His commands, and their moral relevance has nothing to do with His power. God, if omniscient, always makes true judgments about what is to be done by us and what is to be avoided. On this view one might agree with Geach that disobedience will be insane, but one's agreement will be based upon the belief that God always knows best. Then, on those occasions when it appears to us that what is commanded is wrong, we should nevertheless obey: we are apt to be mistaken because our knowledge is finite, but God knows everything there is to be known and can not be mistaken.[23]

Each of these proposed answers is an attempt to avoid what so many writers have seen as the unacceptable consequences of a morality of obedience. Goldstick specifies the believer's self abasement before God as being what gives rise to his commitment to the position that might is right; and Rachels[24] makes a similar claim. But for Geach, God's omnipotence, *all* power as distinct from some high degree of power, renders the believer's attitude somehow more worthy. Swinburne's position can be seen as avoiding the allegedly objectionable lack of reasoning that Nielsen and others identify as the source of the problem for religious moralists.

What is at issue, however, is whether or not one must abandon one's moral autonomy in the act of giving obedience to God on account of some non moral property of His. To act rightly and with moral autonomy, it is felt, one's actions must be based on the conviction that one is doing what is good. Yet neither His omnipotence nor His omniscience appears to guarantee that God's commands will be directed to the good.[25] Geach's position ignores the goodness (or otherwise) of God, while that of Swinburne presupposes it. If I follow Geach then I am, despite what he says, adopting a cringing attitude, albeit one of rational cringing. For I will still have to act against my own judgment as to what is right and wrong (in the case of commands which are objectionable to me) or to act without reference to it (in the case of commands which order or forbid what appears to me to be morally neutral), solely out of the fear of the consequences of disobedience. The guiding principle of my action will be prudential, not moral. Again, if I follow Swinburne, I must take it on trust that God is good, despite appearances to the contrary, if His command is something which I would not normally consider morally acceptable. Recall that the original problem arises, as discussed earlier, from the conviction that one needs to be convinced of the goodness of a rule before one can, morally, obey it.

Yet it may still prove possible to show that some non moral property of God, His omnipotence, in fact, entails His goodness: one can take account both of Geach's emphasis on the distinction between *all* power and *great* power, as well as making room, as Swinburne does, for our powers of reasoning. Then it would not prove necessary to abandon divine command theory by grounding it in the supposed goodness of God.[26] This account of the way in which omnipotence entails goodness will shed a different light upon the problem of making room for autonomy in a moral system which is based on obedience.[27]

First consider the nature of moral autonomy, and the place in morality of prudential action, in a little more detail. The criticisms by Nielsen, MacNamara and others, mentioned above, indicate their conceptions of what it is to be autonomous. To be autonomous is to be self ruling; it is to act upon reasons, rather than mindlessly; it is to make choices for oneself rather than to be swayed wholly by external influences. Autonomy is needed for moral action because it enables us to say that an agent's action is truly *his* action, rather than one which originates from another, and also because it is a precondition for the deliberateness from which moral actions flow. Thus to obey the commands of someone else, whatever those commands may be, would seem to entail an abandonment of autonomy. But is it not possible autonomously to make it a rule for oneself always to follow the commands of someone else?

Two cases need to be distinguished: I may follow another's instructions blindly and unthinkingly, in which case my actions will not be autonomous. But, and quite differently, I may have reasons for obeying the commands of someone else. In many cases these reasons will be prudential, rather than moral. Now what the divine command theorist must show is that he can make it a rule always to follow the commands of someone else (in this case God) while at the same time retaining the autonomy required for moral behaviour, and also that his ultimate reasoning is moral rather than merely prudential, for it is the morality of obedience to divine commands that he wishes to assert. It will not be sufficient for him to show that God always has commanded what is independently seen to be right (that is, that what He commands can be justified on other grounds than that He has commanded it) since the divine command theorist wishes both to make God's commands the basis of morality and also to insist that it would be right to commit oneself to obedience whatever God might command. The objector to divine command theory is in error, however, if he holds that such obedience can at best be only prudential, not moral, claiming that truly moral behaviour would require a knowledge of good which was independent of God's commands (trust which was not based on such knowledge being blind, and any resulting behaviour being non autonomous), or that, though it may be possibly autonomously to commit oneself to a course of action of the kind proposed by the divine command theorist, it would not be possible to remain autonomous once thus committed. For, leaving aside here the earlier argument concerning the nature of faith, the divine command theorist can show that he can pursue his course of action without any independently grounded idea of goodness, that his autonomy can be maintained, and that his actions are morally right.

One can commit oneself to obeying God now and always on prudential grounds without abandoning one's autonomy, in so far as that consists in reasoning things out for oneself. For if He is omnipotent then, as Geach argues, it is insane to disobey Him: no real benefit could ever come of it; great disaster would come of it (assuming the correctness of the traditional theistic account of Hell). And if one assumes, reasonably enough, that He will always continue to be omnipotent, then it always will be insane to disobey Him. Thus one always has reasons, the most pressing of reasons in fact, for continued obedience. Disobedience could only be the course of the weak, the irrational, the ill informed etc., and so obedience is entirely consistent with autonomy conceived of as rational self directedness. This holds regardless of whether one has any knowledge of what is morally good. What remains to be established is how such prudential behaviour, how self interested obedience, is to be accounted moral.

But what is 'moral' supposed to mean? If morality is objective,[28] then even an atheistic opponent of divine command morality must accept that this objectivity entails that there is something which he can be mistaken about; that what is really right is so independently of whether he happens to think it right; that his deepest convictions could be wrong; that on discovering his error he would have to revise his behaviour in such a way that he then acted in a manner he would not autonomously have chosen beforehand. He has, that is, just the same problem which he sees as a crucial difficulty for divine command theory: in order to do what is objectively right he might have to compromise his autonomy. The objector to divine command theory considers that the problem over autonomy arises in part because God could command what we now believe to be wrong, yet we ought, if the theory were correct, to obey such commands. But this is true for *any* objective morality. As Clark remarks:

> If God's commands cannot be the source of moral duty (on the plea that it might be the case that He commanded something now believed to be wrong), then even the moral law itself (considered as something independent even of God's action) cannot be the source of moral duty. Which is clearly absurd.[29]

The threat, if it is a threat, to autonomy stems only from the objectivity of morality, not from its nature as rooted either in God's will or in His command. Bambrough, discussing Hare's view, remarks that on his account

> we must be free to form our opinions on moral qualities in some sense in which we are not free to form our opinions on matters of fact and matters of logic... The stress is on the individuality and autonomy of the response that is required of the moral agent.[30]

But of course, that conception of autonomous moral action is precisely what moral objectivists deny: the distinction between matters of morals and matters of fact is, for them, a false one.

Consider now Dworkin's remarks on moral autonomy:

The most general formulation of moral autonomy is: A person is morally autonomous if and only if his moral principles are his own. The following are more specific characterizations of what it might mean for moral principles to be one's own.

1. A person is morally autonomous if and only if he is the author of his moral principles, their originator.
2. A person is morally autonomous if and only if he chooses his moral principles.
3. A person is morally autonomous if and only if the ultimate authority or source of his moral principles is his will.
4. A person is morally autonomous if and only if he decides which moral principles to accept as binding upon him.
5. A person is morally autonomous if and only if he bears the responsibility for the moral theory he accepts and the principles he applies.
6. A person is morally autonomous if and only if he refuses to accept others as moral authorities, that is, he does not accept without independent consideration the judgment of others as to what is morally correct.[31]

Dworkin makes some telling points in his assessment of these suggested definitions. The first four, he says, are incompatible with moral objectivity; the fifth is true but vacuous; and the sixth neglects the reliance upon authority which is common in other areas. He also notes that a conception of morality which stresses autonomy is liable to encounter problems over accounting for obligation. Rejecting the suggestion that obligation can be self imposed, he says that 'This attempted solution cannot succeed. Tying oneself up is binding only if the knot is no longer in one's hands. For if I can, at will, release myself I am only in appearance bound'.[32]

Young[33] terms 'external negative constraints' upon autonomy those factors which he considers reduce autonomy, factors which entail that certain options I might choose or want to choose are not available to me. Moral objectivity amounts to just such a factor: I can not carry out a morally good theft if external considerations entail that theft can not be good. But one must be careful not to confuse autonomy with freedom. Bearing in mind Dworkin's remarks, let us say rather that I act autonomously if what I choose is deliberately and rationally chosen by me. Then Young is incorrect when he argues, for instance, that poverty inhibits autonomy, and that abject poverty can even destroy it. What matters is that from the range of things that I can choose, what is chosen for me is chosen by me, and chosen, it should be stressed again, deliberately and rationally. It is no constraint upon my autonomy that I can not choose to fly to the moon or to buy a yacht: rather, those are constraints on my freedom. Similarly, the existence of external objective values (whether in morality or in other areas) may be said to constrain my freedom (I am not free to make an action right by wishing it so or by believing it so; no more am I free to make the laws of logic untrue by believing them so) but it in no way inhibits my autonomy. Granted, there is something over which I have no control, but it is not my behaviour: rather, it is the rightness of my behaviour. Whatever the source of moral obligation (assuming again that morality is objective) there will be some constraints on me, in the sense that I will have duties that I do not choose; but I can still choose whether to act in accordance with external obligations, *whether to do my duty*. That I do not agree that an action is wrong is, on any objective account of morality, wholly unconnected with the fact that it is wrong: my autonomy is not relevant here.

Placing oneself at the disposal of another and consenting always to obey his commands need not then entail any abandonment of autonomy, for there can be well considered reasons for such a course of action. If the foregoing argument is accepted, it is not in relation to autonomy that accounts such as Geach's and Swinburne's fail, but rather in their ascription to the moral agent of an inappropriate motive for action. But if one does indeed have a way of demonstrating that God's commands must be good then one's moral motivation will not be compromised.

Omnipotence and goodness

Consider next how it can be shown that omnipotence entails goodness. Goldstick notes that the theist's claim, that it is necessarily the case that whatever God should will is good, is equivalent to the claim that there could not be an omnipotent demon.[34] (This can be accepted, for although someone who occasionally or only once wills something bad would not perhaps be considered a demon, the willing by God of what was immoral, even on one occasion only, could be sufficient for Him to be in all relevant respects like an omnipotent demon, since His one act of badness could be so fundamental as to be equal in its effects to repeated demonic acts. For instance, He could maliciously have neglected to inform us that the whole body of scripture should, for it to be correct, have been preceded by the words, 'It is not the case that'.) Then if it can be shown that an omnipotent demon is actually an impossibility, the theist's claim will be vindicated.

What would an omnipotent demon be like? Before answering this question it would be necessary to know whether or not what was good and bad was so independently of the demon. Just as in the case of God it can be supposed that the existence of a criterion of goodness which was independent of Him would constitute a limitation upon His power[35] (for there would be something over which He had no control; something which He might, conceivably, wish to be other than it was, but which He could not alter), so too the demon would not be genuinely omnipotent unless he were free from such constraints as would be implied by the independent existence of a moral criterion (as would be implied, for that matter, by the existence of anything whatever that was independent of him). It will not do to argue, either in the case of God or of the demon, that what is good or bad is, while not independent of the omnipotent being, nevertheless something over which it has no control: it might be said, for example, that goodness (or badness) inheres in the nature of God (or of the demon). But this would amount in God's case to saying that He could not but be good; and this in turn entails, in the absence of any independent criterion of goodness, that whatever God should happen to do would, just by virtue of its being His deed, be good. And if it is just His doing a deed which makes it good, and if the deeds He does are under His control, as must be the case for an omnipotent being, then what is good is after all something over which He has control. To suggest that goodness is in some way bound up with God's nature, where this suggestion is intended as a way of showing that, though nothing exists independently of God, He yet has no control over what constitutes goodness, is no less a denial of His omnipotence than is the outright claim that there does exist a criterion of goodness which is independent of Him. For to separate God's nature from His will in such a way that the former is not subject to the latter entails, even though it preserves the idea that nothing exists independently from God, that He is not omnipotent. (God may, perhaps, necessarily will what is good as a matter of logic - that is, it could turn out to be a logical truth that whatever God wills is good; or it could be a truth of language - God could be good by definition. But neither of these possibilities is relevant to His omnipotence or to the question whether anything exists independently of Him). It can therefore be concluded that if God is omnipotent then what is good or bad depends on His will.

What applies to Almighty God in virtue of His omnipotence will also apply, *mutatis mutandis*, to the omnipotent demon. What is good or bad will be in some manner dependent on his will. Then how exactly will his behaviour be demonic? Consider the following suggestions:

1. The demon decides what is to be called good and what is to be called bad, and then acts in such a way that all of his deeds fall into the latter category.

2. The demon creates a universe which includes a world inhabited by humans; he determines what sort of human behaviour will lead to human well being, and then proceeds to arrange things in such a way that whatever people do, they can not attain their well being.

3. The demon inflicts pain on his creatures; he tortures animals and humans, causing them continual distress.

But in order for the demon to make an action or class of actions bad, in order for him to will that this be the case, something more must be involved than the mere assignation to actions of arbitrary labels. For otherwise the demon would be doing just that - arbitrarily naming actions, and this process of naming would not carry with it any implications about what was to be done or avoided. To say that an action is good or bad in a moral sense is to do more than simply to give it a name: it is to say something about whether that action ought to be done (though this should not be taken as an endorsement of prescriptivism - it is to say that and more). So when the demon classifies actions according to their moral status he must have in mind that those which he calls good are those which are to be done, and that those which he calls bad are those which are to be avoided. And when it is said that the demon wills that an action is to be done or is to be avoided, this presumably means that the demon wants that action done or avoided. There may be contexts in which it is desirable to maintain a distinction between willing and wanting, but this is not one of them. For our purpose here it seems clear that intending that something be the case may accurately be said to include both willing it so and wanting it so. Then the first case envisaged above, where the demon acts in an evil manner entirely on his own, in the absence of any creation, will not be a possibility. It makes no sense to suppose that an omnipotent being can want some action to be avoided and then proceed to do it, or want some action to be done and then proceed to avoid it: behaviour of this sort is explicable only when action is in some way restricted or coerced, but an omnipotent being can not be subject to restriction or coercion. Alternatively, such behaviour may not be explicable at all, for it may be quite irrational. But presumably an omnipotent being will be rational: irrationality implies a deficiency that is incompatible with the possession of all power. If, therefore, an omnipotent being wants a particular state of affairs to obtain then it is certain that its want will be realized, and that the state of affairs will obtain.

In the second case, it would be an error to imagine that, since the demon continually frustrates people's attempts to achieve what is 'good for them', he thereby does wrong. For the following argument shows that it could not be wrong to frustrate human endeavours in that way, no matter what they were directed towards.

On the face of it, it might seem clear that a creator who intervened in human affairs in such a way that, for example, eating food which was necessary for survival always caused illnesses which impeded survival, would be acting in an evil manner. But this seems obvious only because it is assumed that survival is a good while illness is an evil. When it is recalled, however, that goods and evils are determined by the demon creator to be good or evil, and that they are good or evil for no other reason than that he so arranges matters, the position is seen to be rather different. If survival is a human good, and if illness is a human evil, then what the demon has determined is this: that it ought to be the case that humans survive, and that it ought not to be the case that humans fall ill. Then human survival and freedom from illness are states of affairs which are willed by the creator. This being the case, the demon's interventions in human affairs could not, on pain of contradiction (that is, he would have to will both a state of affairs and its opposite), be directed towards the hindrance of survival, or towards the promotion of illness. To the extent that demonic intervention did in fact hinder survival or bring about illness, bearing in mind that the consequences of intervention could not (on account of the demon's having power over all things) be accidental or unforeseen, one would have to admit that in such cases the demon willed differently, and that therefore, on these occasions, illness and the hindrance of survival were good things.

Similar considerations apply in the third case. If torture and pain really are evils, in a world in which what is evil (by which is meant, in the situation envisaged, what is to be avoided) is nothing other than *what the omnipotent creator wishes to be avoided*, then the demon can not consistently inflict them on his creatures. The outcome of this is that the omnipotent demon can do no wrong. More accurately, there can not be an omnipotent demon if his omnipotence entails that there be no criterion of right and wrong which is independent of him. Then the fact that an omnipotent being can do no wrong does not constitute a constraint on its power, since its inability to do wrong is a logical consequence of its omnipotence.[36] Rather, what is implied is that, although he can do anything at all, it will never be correct to describe what he does as evil. This illustration does more than show, circularly, that if goodness is just to mean or to be whatever God wills then He can do no wrong; for it highlights the reason why nothing but goodness can issue from an omnipotent being, when omnipotence ranges over the moral status of truths. That something is good carries the implication that in some circumstance it ought to be so; that an action is good implies that in some circumstance it ought to be done.[37] It is not therefore an arbitrary matter whether we equate the actions of an omnipotent being with badness rather than goodness. If goodness is *what ought to be* then omnipotent God must be good; and if goodness is not *what ought to be* then the result is a confusion, and incoherence.

Suppose that the theist accepts the foregoing argument, and believes that God's omnipotence guarantees that He can do no wrong. It does not follow that this belief entails a commitment to, or just is, a belief that might is right. The two beliefs are not the same at all. The acceptance of an argument such as that given above, to the effect that an omnipotent being can not, logically, do wrong, does not entail the further acceptance of the proposition that might *per se* guarantees that its possessor is righteous, or that righteousness is proportional to might, or any similar such proposition. For what is crucial in the account of the connection between omnipotence and righteousness is not that a being who is omnipotent has *great* power but that he has *all* power.[38] The existence of a very mighty being does not preclude the existence of an even mightier being. Satan may have great power, but if the being who is mightier than he is happens to be Almighty God, who makes the moral law, then Satan's strength implies no righteousness. On the other hand, the existence of an omnipotent being does preclude the existence of any other being of greater power.

Still, it might be felt that, though it has been established that God's righteousness can be due to His omnipotence in such a way that no equation of right with might need be made, there is nevertheless nothing attractive about all powerfulness, given that powerfulness is not in itself a quality which demands admiration or moral praise. It is possibly this feeling of unease which accounts for the readiness of opponents of divine command theory to dismiss it as being tantamount to power worship, and as such morally reprehensible. But this misgiving is unfounded: quite apart from the fact that God's power carries with it none of the possibilities for abuse that accompany so much worldly power (for it can not, logically, be abused), the admiration or attraction which, it is felt, ought to be directed towards God on account of His qualities can indeed be directed towards Him with perfect propriety. For it is as a perfection that God's all powerfulness can be admired, rather than as an abundance of strength, if it is thought that strength is not an especially admirable quality. A comparison may help to make the point: if I hear that someone has won a golf tournament, say, then it is feasible that I should not be the least bit impressed, since I may have no interest in golf and no admiration for any of the skills involved in playing it; but if I hear that the same person has for the past five years won every trophy without exception at national and international level, then notwithstanding my lack of interest in golf, it could prove difficult to be unimpressed. The idea of being unequalled, of being the complete master of a skill, of exceptionless, high calibre performance with respect to some quality, can perhaps attract and stimulate admiration where simple consideration of the quality alone leaves one unmoved.

Conclusion

On the divine command account, not only can there *be* no conflict between right and duty (whatever duty God should choose to lay down), but there can be no *perceived* conflict in mind of the believer.[39] The suggestion that a morally acceptable motive is present when an action is done because it is right, but absent when an action is performed because omnipotent God commands it, relies upon a distinction which is not admitted by the theist who holds an Ockhamist conception of God's power. There is, for him, no account of what it is to be right other than the account which says that to be right is to be as God wills it. For him, these are not two distinct properties, but are one and the same. It is true that the two can be conceived separately, but that ceases to be so when the full implications of divine omnipotence are taken into account. It then becomes implausible to argue that motivation is adequate in so far as it relates to a divine property under one description, but not when it relates to the very same property under another description. In effect, in the context of obedience to divine commands, prudence and morality are indistinguishable (the contrast between prudence and morality in other circumstances makes sense only because it could be the case that the prudent and the moral should fail to coincide).[40] Further, in acknowledging God's power over the status of moral truths the believer makes God's commands his own, as it were, in just the same manner as any other autonomous moral agent. As Gascoigne puts it:

To obey ethical imperatives expressed as God's will through revelation and tradition is not to bow to sheer authority in defiance or neglect of autonomous ethical judgement, but rather to identify divine will as perceived through religion with divine will as the origin of creation.[41]

Religious believers do more than simply *recognize* morality in God's will: 'Religion is the *attachment* to an ultimate and fundamental demand'.[42] It no longer makes sense to suppose that a believer might be required by divine command to do something wrong or objectionable. It remains true, of course, that he does not choose his moral principles; but then it is quite incredible to claim that such a choice is available even to the most extreme moral subjectivist. If an emotivist finds the practice of slavery morally repugnant, he can not by act of will choose to like it; he can not choose, that is, to find it morally acceptable, as and when he likes. Choice does not enter into the matter.

Nothing in the foregoing argument amounts to a denial of the importance of personal moral autonomy. Rather, what has been argued is that the relevant objections to divine command morality are misdirected: the obedient creature does not compromise his personal autonomy, and those matters which are outside the scope of his choice are put beyond his reach by the objective nature of morality, not by its nature as rooted in obedience to his Creator. I may obey, say, the precepts of the decalogue and do so by choice because I believe that to be the right course of action. I may also believe that it is the right course of action only because it accords with God's will. If personal moral autonomy is conceived of as a form of self rule in moral matters, this must not be taken to mean that the autonomous agent also rules the world of objective facts. I rule myself in moral matters when I act freely and out of conviction, not when I choose what things I shall regard as right or wrong.

Notes

1 *Catechism of the Catholic Church* (1994), Vatican, sections 268-9, p. 63.
2 See his *Super Quattuor Libros Sententiarum* (1495), in *Opera Plurima*, vols. 3 and 4, Lyons; facsimile reprint (1962), Gregg Press: London.
3 Copleston (1953), *A History of Philosophy*, vol. 3, London, p. 105.
4 Op. cit., section 270, p. 64. The quotation in this section is from Aquinas's *Summa Theologiae*, Ia, 25, 5.
5 Johnson (1990), *A History of Christianity*, Penguin Books: London, p. 14.
6 The point can be phrased differently to avoid such complications. One could talk instead of God (timelessly) making p and -p true simultaneously.

7   *Summa Theologiae*, Ia, 25, 3. See too Swinburne (1974), 'Duty and the Will of God', *Canadian Journal of Philosophy* IV, 2, pp. 213-27; also Swinburne (1973), 'Omnipotence', *American Philosophical Quarterly* 10, pp. 231-7; and Kenny (1988), *The God of the Philosophers*, Oxford, particularly chapter VII, 'The Definition of Omnipotence'.

8   Lewis (1988), *The Problem of Pain*, Fount Paperbacks, p. 22. There have been opponents of this view. Shestov, reacting against Leibniz's view that necessary truths were necessary independently of God, argues that a God who is subject to the laws of logic is not the God of the Bible for whom all things are possible. He takes the story of Job to mean that God is not subject to the law of non contradiction, since He revises time in such a way that Job both has and has not his children. His account is discussed in Wernham (1968), *Two Russian Thinkers*, Toronto. Also, Descartes (see the translation of his correspondence with Mersenne, in Kenny (1970), *Philosophical Letters*, Oxford) suggests that God could have created a different order of necessary truths from the order which actually obtains, and that though we are now bound, as it were, by the logic that does obtain, things could yet have been otherwise. However, if we are to avoid denying our reason altogether, then not only must we accept that the law of non contradiction *is* true, but we must also accept that it could not but be true. There is no sense in supposing that what is nonsense-to-us is not *really* nonsense: we can give no intelligible content to the notions of 'real nonsense' and 'nonsense-to-us' in any way that allows a distinction to be made between them. See too Goldstick (1990), 'Could God make a Contradiction True?', *Religious Studies* 26, pp. 377-87.

9   Quinn (1978), *Divine Commands and Moral Requirements*, Clarendon Press: Oxford, p. 38.

10 Quinn (1990), 'An Argument for Divine Command Ethics', in Beaty, *Christian Theism and The Problems of Philosophy*, University of Notre Dame Press, p. 293.

11 Cf. McCabe (1980), 'God II: Freedom', *New Blackfriars*, pp. 456-69. This point raises problems of free will which are beyond the scope of this work.

12 Matthew 5;48.

13 'When people have tried to read into "God can do everything" a signification not of Pious Intention but of Philosophical Truth, they have only landed themselves in intractable problems and hopeless confusions; no graspable sense has ever been given to this sentence that did not lead to self-contradiction or at least to conclusions manifestly untenable from the Christian point of view' - Geach (1977), *Providence and Evil*, Cambridge, p. 4. His arguments are discussed in Flint and Freddoso

(1987), 'Maximal Power', in Morris, *The Concept of God*, Oxford University Press: Oxford, pp. 134-67.
14   See Mackie (1955), 'Evil and Omnipotence', *Mind* 64, pp. 200-212; Plantinga (1967), *God and Other Minds*, Ithaca; Swinburne (1977), *The Coherence of Theism*, Oxford; Pearl (1986), 'The Misuse of Anselm's Formula for God's Perfection', *Religious Studies* 22, pp. 355-65.
15   Van den Brink (1992), *Almighty God: A Study of the Doctrine of Divine Omnipotence*, Utrecht, p. 132.
16   Nielsen (1973), *Ethics Without God*, London, p. 3.
17   MacNamara (1991), 'Ethics Human and Christian', in Freyne, *Ethics and The Christian*, Columba Press: Dublin, p. 86.
18   Daly (1991), 'Conscience, Guilt and Sin', in Freyne, op. cit., pp. 59-60.
19   Nowell-Smith (1966), 'Morality: Religious and Secular', in Ramsey, *Christian Ethics and Contemporary Philosophy*, London, p. 97. See also the criticism of Nowell-Smith in Mouw (1990), *The God Who Commands*, University of Notre Dame Press, p. 12.
20   Meynell (1994), *Is Christianity True?*, London, p. 24.
21   Goldstick (1974), 'Monotheism's Euthyphro Problem', *Canadian Journal of Philosophy* 3, pp. 585-89.
22   Geach (1981), 'The Moral Law and The Law of God', in Helm, *Divine Commands and Morality*, Oxford University Press: Oxford, p. 173.
23   Swinburne (1974), 'Duty and the Will of God'.
24   Rachels (1971), 'God and Human Attitudes', *Religious Studies* 7, pp. 325-37.
25   Similar arguments apply in cases where it is held that obedience is owed to God on account of His being our owner or father. See Brody (1981), 'Morality and Religion Reconsidered' and Phillips (1981), 'God and Ought', both in Helm (1981), op. cit.
26   Grounding it in His love also results in the abandonment of the theory: if divine commands are only to be obeyed because they are issued by a *loving* God, then presumably what is commanded is right not simply because God has ordered it; rather, He has ordered it because it is right. In this connection see the two articles by Adams which are cited in the introduction, as well as Clark (1982), 'God's Law and Morality', *Philosophical Quarterly* 32, pp. 339-47; Clark (1987), 'Discussion: God's Law and Chandler', *Philosophical Quarterly* 37, pp. 203-8; Chandler (1985), 'Clark on God's Law and Morality', *Philosophical Quarterly* 35, pp. 87-90; and Quinn (1990), 'The Recent Revival of Divine Command Ethics', *Philosophy and Phenomenological Research* 1, supplement, pp. 345-65. There are in any case difficulties in accounting for God's love - this is discussed later.

27 See Mahoney (1968), 'Obedience: Consent or Conformity?', *The Way*, supplement no. 6, pp. 5-19.
28 Moral objectivity is presupposed. I have indicated the reasoning behind this presupposition in the introduction.
29 Clark (1987), op. cit.
30 Bambrough (1979), *Moral Scepticism and Moral Knowledge*, London, pp. 81-2. The account he discusses is in Hare (1963), *Freedom and Reason*, Oxford University Press.
31 Dworkin (1988), *The Theory and Practice of Autonomy*, Cambridge University Press: Cambridge, pp. 34-5.
32 Dworkin, op. cit., p. 42.
33 Young (1986), *Personal Autonomy*, London, pp. 46-7.
34 Goldstick (1974), op. cit.
35 This position is discussed and argued for in more depth later. Here it is merely outlined and taken for granted.
36 In this connection see Pike (1969), 'Omnipotence and God's Ability to Sin', *American Philosophical Quarterly* 6, pp. 208-16; and Brown (1991), 'God's Ability to Will Moral Evil', *Faith and Philosophy* 8, pp. 3-20.
37 Anscombe may be correct to hold that our moral language is in this respect a left over from an earlier, religious age. But a Christian could agree with that point while still denying that the religious basis which connects goodness and obligation had lost its relevance: religion is still, after all, alive and well; and atheistic moralists might yet want to argue that moral qualities give rise to obligations. See her (1958) 'Modern Moral Philosophy', *Philosophy* 33, pp. 1-19. See too: MacIntyre (1981), *After Virtue*, Duckworth: London; and the arguments (particularly chapter two) in Sacks (1991), *The Persistence of Faith*, London.
38 The importance of this point is overlooked by Karl Barth in his (1957) *Church Dogmatics*, Edinburgh.
39 Cf. the view of Evagrius Ponticus: 'A healthy soul is not one which grimly does its duty, it is one which is doing what it wants to do' (and still doing its duty). Cited in Tugwell (1984), *Ways of Imperfection: An Exploration of Christian Spirituality*, Darton Longman and Todd: London, p. 29.
40 See also Williams (1972), *Morality: An Introduction to Ethics*, Cambridge University Press: Cambridge, pp. 77-86.
41 Gascoigne (1985), 'God and Objective Moral Values', *Religious Studies* 21, pp. 531-49.
42 Murdoch (1993), *Metaphysics as a Guide to Morals*, Penguin Books: London, p. 146.

4 Natural law, reason and conscience

Introduction

In addition to the opposition to divine command morality that comes from those who altogether deny the possibility of religious morality, there has been, and remains, much opposition to it in its Christian form among Christians themselves. This Christian opposition to a moral system based upon the revealed commands of God may take shape in various ways, but generally what these have in common is a conviction that some things which are good or right in the area of human activity could not but be good or right. So it may be held that, while there is a religious aspect to morality, for example in that a wise and loving God guides us by His commandments towards an awareness of moral truths, or in that Jesus is the moral role model *par excellence*, God's expressed will is nevertheless not in itself what constitutes the foundations of morality. Such an account may be offered either in the conviction that we just do not need divine commands in order to know our moral duty because we can work out what, for reasons unconnected with divine commands, it must be; or in the belief that God can not make right what is now wrong: He forbids murder, adultery and theft because these are wrong, and He could not command us to commit any of these wrongs, because He is good and loving. A more or less central role may be accorded to revelation by such a Christian opponent of divine command theory, but whatever importance is attached to it, the revealed word of God will not be basic to morality in the sense that, as His word, the expression of His will, it *makes* right what is right; though it may be basic in some other way, for instance by expressing what is, for reasons unconnected to or independent of God's will, the set of primary moral precepts.

Two traditions are prominent here, that of natural law morality and that of Christian Platonism. This chapter is concerned with the first of these traditions, and the following chapter with the second. I propose to show, through an examination of arguments typical of each, that the opposition to divine command theory expressed by the Christian natural law theorist and the Christian Platonist is unjustified, and that divine commands actually constitute a better basis, better, that is, in terms of Christian morality generally, than is often thought to be the case.

Natural law

It is almost a commonplace that one can not infer one's moral duties merely from examining the way the world is, that one can not infer moral values from sheer physical facts.[1] But natural law theory as considered here does not involve, once its presuppositions are made clear, any obviously invalid inference from facts to values:[2] that something is a good is taken for granted; value is presupposed in the premises of the arguments which derive our duties from considering what we are like. For example, an atheistic formulation of natural law such as that of Hart is based on the assumption that it is a good thing for a man to pursue happiness.[3] It is worth considering the differences which must exist between Hart's account and any account of natural law which is to be distinctively Christian, since they are relevant to what is at issue between the Christian who espouses natural law morality and his fellow believer who favours divine command morality.

First, and most obviously, Christian moral theory emphasizes the importance of man's duties to God; second, it stresses the value of the happiness of people other than oneself, a value which any agent must take account of in practical decisions; third, it insists upon the existence of an objective happiness which is quite independent of whatever we may happen to think our happiness consists in: happiness is not merely pleasure, and it is something about which we can be mistaken.

The first of these differences is relatively clear; the second and third can be illustrated as follows:

First, on an account such as Hart's, which involves constructing a set of moral precepts which will regulate man's behaviour so as to enable the pursuit of happiness to take place, an agent will indeed take into consideration the effects of his actions upon others, but only to the extent that is required for the pursuit of self interest. From the fact that the satisfaction of my interest is something I see as good, together with a recognition that all people are similar in this respect, I can not infer that another's interest is something which I ought to help satisfy. All I can validly infer is that some other person will want to satisfy his interests as I do my own. Mitchell says, of the Kantian method of extending one's principle of action to include others, that all Kant really shows is that 'the agent be prepared to be consistent in his choices and make the same demands upon himself as upon anyone else similarly situated', and that this is not enough for the derivation of a moral system.[4] But although Kant does not even show as much as Mitchell credits him with showing (for my choices concerning the satisfaction of my interests do not, as has been said earlier, result from their being the interests of a rational being, nor indeed from their being the interests of any particular sort of being, but from their being mine[5]), Mitchell's point is still relevant: bare consistency, the mere following of the Golden Rule, is possible while admitting a wide range of actions including those which many moralists, whether Christian or not, would wish to condemn;[6] a sado-masochist can follow the Golden Rule. It might be objected here that the force of Kant's argument is stronger than I allow: an agent could not act on the maxim that stealing was acceptable while simultaneously willing that his maxim should be a universal one, for then the result would be a subversion of the concept of property upon which stealing depends. This consequence may indeed follow, but it is not relevant. For if I steal, and allow it as universally acceptable, the logical consequences for the concepts involved are not such as to make my actions rationally unacceptable. If I take a neighbour's car and am prepared to allow such behaviour universally I commit no logical error, and my neighbour is still lacking his car.[7]

Second, a moral system based upon natural law alone can use no criterion for what is happiness making other than what is found by observation to make people happy. If goodness is identified with the happiness people achieve, then even with the further stipulation that such happiness must not detract from that of others, so that, for example, the practice of sado-masochism will no longer be accounted good, the result will be a conception of goodness which is wholly at odds with the Christian conception of goodness. For on this latter account, what one takes to be happiness does not become genuine happiness, and pleasurable activity does not become acceptable activity, simply because it harms no one else.

Consider the example of a community of people living together, men and women and their children, in much the same way as the traditional family - one man, one wife, and their children - lives together. The community envisaged here has no strict rules about the sexual partnerships its members, if adults, may engage in. Thus one man may father children by a number of women, and one woman may bear the children of a number of men. Suppose further that the relationships between all the members are based on mutual love and support, that the children are properly cared for, and that the prevailing ethos is one of altruistic benevolence and concern for the common good, including the good of non members. From the point of view of natural law nothing is amiss in this community: people are pursuing and, let it be supposed, achieving happiness. Even from the point of view of one who supplements natural law with a - possibly divinely inspired/revelation based - concern for the welfare of others, a genuine altruism, nothing is amiss. For there is no natural law conception of happiness other than what in fact makes people happy; there is nothing to be observed in the world which informs us that happiness *ought* to consist in such and such behaviour, and that thinking we are happy is not the measure of real happiness.

The Christian, however, might point out that the life of the community envisaged here is based on institutionalized fornication or adultery, and that monogamy *should* prevail whether or not polygamy appears pleasurable and harmless. He might, of course, add that the behaviour of the community will, in the long term, result in the unhappiness of its members, since he believes that defying the will of God will incur punishment. But apart from the inadmissibility of this as a *moral* argument (it may well be a compelling *prudential* argument) it is a larger claim than can be supported by considerations of natural law. Since there is no observation which can be made in confirmation of the Christian's conception of the after life, from the point of view of natural law he has gone beyond what the data supplied by nature entitle him to. Unless it is an observable fact that the behaviour considered by the Christian to be immoral causes unhappiness then he is not entitled to say that it is wrong according to natural law.[8] Similarly, if (for example) homosexual activity always brought fire and brimstone (or ill health) in its wake, it could be condemned on natural law grounds. And if one knew from observation that it resulted in damnation then one would be prudent in avoiding it. But it is not observably followed by bad consequences, and could not therefore be thus condemned. Knowledge of the existence and nature of an after life might hugely alter any theory of morality, but such knowledge is not available from observation.

Lest it be thought at this point that the emphasis on happiness has the result that natural law theory is identified too closely with some form of utilitarianism, it should be explained why happiness has such an important role in natural law morality. If one is trying to determine whether something is functioning properly, working as it ought to work, then it is necessary to bear in mind what its function aims at. In natural law morality inferences are made about the way one ought to act from observations of what humans are in fact like; and distinctions are drawn between human conditions which are ordered correctly and those which are ordered wrongly. However, as noted above, certain premises concerning value are presupposed: account is taken not only of what things *are* like but of what they *must be* like if the world is to continue in a certain way. So a properly functioning bodily organ is one that is working in the manner required for physical health; and in order to determine what constitutes a person's health, one needs to have a conception of the aim or end of the functioning of a human body. It seems that the least controversial end that can be ascribed to human activity is human happiness: it is not only mere survival that is sought, but survival which includes something that makes it worthwhile. This need not be taken to imply that there is any moral obligation to pursue happiness as an end, but amounts to no more than the claim that human flourishing or well being must include the pursuit or achievement of happiness in order properly to be so called. Presumably it is less controversial to say, for instance, that a person who survives happily is somehow functioning better than someone who is merely surviving, than it would be to put the claim the other way around.

St. Thomas Aquinas took the view that the duty to marry no more than one spouse was something one could deduce from the duty to propagate the species, this latter duty being derivable from natural law.[9] Enlarging on that claim, Rickaby observes that the practical results of polygamy and polyandry are such as to detract from the proper upbringing of the issue: if polyandry is permitted, 'no man can ever know his own child, except by likeness, and likeness in a baby face is largely as you choose to fancy it'; if polygamy is permitted, then the natural bond of affection between man and wife is weakened.[10] Although these claims can be disputed or even dismissed outright as false, what is important is that the case against multiple spouses in natural law, as it is conceived by, for instance, the Thomist, is a conditional one: *if* polygamy is detrimental to what natural law requires in the way of rearing offspring *then* it is itself contrary to natural law. If it could be shown to Aquinas's satisfaction that the community in the above example made adequate provision for bringing up children then doubtless he would consider the arrangements to be no infringement of natural law.[11] He is at pains to stress that natural law does not consist in reason operating in the abstract, but involves the application of reason to facts about the world. For example, in the matter of adultery, his view is put by Copleston as follows:

> As regards deduction, Aquinas did not think that we can deduce the proposition that to have sexual intercourse with someone else's wife is wrong from the precept that good is to be pursued and evil avoided simply by contemplating, as it were, this latter precept... The concrete good for man can be known only by reflection on human nature as known in experience.[12]

Natural law does not, then, operate in a vacuum. A Christian version of natural law requires the support of distinctively Christian premises. That this is so is not always made clear: Farrell, expounding Aquinas, writes that in the matter of conforming our will to the will of God,

> a special revelation of God's intentions is not necessary; it is not necessary that we have a blueprint of all the detailed devices of divine providence; we do not have to spend agonizing hours on our knees trying to discover if this is or is not the will of God. We have only to follow our reason.[13]

It would be too easy to read into this remark a denial of the importance of both scripture and prayer. Though natural law morality can be presented in such a way that it is wholly antithetical to divine command morality, such an opposition is not a necessary one. It is possible to present an account of morality which stresses the ultimate importance of divine commands, while retaining an important place for natural law and being thoroughly Christian in nature. Farrell, it may be noted, is a Dominican, as was Aquinas. He presumably shares what Battaglia says is the chief presupposition of Aquinas's outlook, that is, 'that one begins talking of 'truth', 'law', etc., in the certainty that one is dealing with a universe that a Creator has created good. The focus of Thomas' attention is this Creator and this world thus assured of goodness'.[14] In other words, the Thomist's emphasis on natural law must be viewed alongside his conviction that God is the author of all goodness. Aquinas is insistent that natural law is not in itself a sufficient basis for morality; and Farrell's remark must be seen as a denial, not of the relevance of scripture, but of the need for scriptural support, or for explicit revelation, in all the details of day to day moral decision making. Thus Aquinas writes,

> The planning of human life required, over and above the law we have by nature and the human laws we make, law made by God. For men are destined for an eternal happiness which lies beyond their natural powers of achievement, and so they needed God to give them laws that could help them plan for that goal,

and when men's judgments differ, they need God 'to give them an infallible law to guide them'.[15]

Copleston notes, too, that according to Aquinas, a proper knowledge of God can not be attained by us in this life, and that revelation is necessary in order to show both that such knowledge is ultimately attainable (after death, that is) and also that it is the actual end of this life, the correct thing to work towards.[16]

A Christian version of natural law morality can not, then, dispense with the need for revealed truths concerning the will of God, not least because the Christian believes in, but has no empirical knowledge of, an after life.[17] Nor, of course, can the divine command moralist dispense with the requirement to apply his reason, in conjunction with his knowledge of the world in general and his experience of human nature in particular, to the processes of using divine commands in concrete situations where their relevance is not clear or straightforward, and of inferring the divine will from what he knows both of the world and of the commands contained in scripture. In effect, he must apply his knowledge of natural law to divine commands, while the natural law theorist must apply his knowledge (including his knowledge of divine commands) to his experience of nature. The two theories are not necessarily equivalent on this account, since they may differ greatly in their emphasis, but they are much closer than is sometimes thought.

Apart from the sheer inadequacy of reason alone, or of reason applied to nature, in the matter of formulating a specifically Christian moral system, there are further practical and commonsense considerations which the Christian moralist must take into account in his assessment of the function in morality of revealed truths. Butler observes that 'no revelation would have been given, had the light of nature been sufficient... to render one... useless'.[18] The remarks of Chesterton on this subject are apposite too:

> St. Thomas takes the view that the souls of all the ordinary hardworking and simple-minded people are quite as important as the souls of thinkers and truth-seekers; and he asks how all these people are possibly to find time for the amount of reasoning that is needed to find truth. The whole tone... shows both a respect for scientific enquiry and a strong sympathy with the average man. His argument for Revelation is not an argument against Reason; but it is an argument for Revelation. The conclusion he draws from it is that men must receive the highest moral truths in a miraculous manner; or most men would not receive them at all.[19]

He adds:

> in the matter of the inspiration of Scripture, he [Aquinas] fixed first on the obvious fact, which was forgotten by four furious centuries of sectarian battle, that the meaning of Scripture is very far from self-evident; and that we must often interpret it in the light of other truths. If a literal interpretation is really and flatly contradicted by an obvious fact, why then we can only say that the literal interpretation must be a false interpretation. But the fact must really be an obvious fact.[20]

Reason is important, but can not dispense with the need for revelation.[21]

It needs to be stressed that a synthesis of revelation and reason, of scripture and natural law, is not a step towards moral relativism. The revelation which is relevant here is that in scripture which concerns morality: it is, in effect, divine commands. Now the divine command theorist would be rightly alarmed if the content of divine commands were to be ignored, or distorted, or relativized, on the basis that they must somehow be made to conform to the natural law. But a synthesis of divine commands and natural law need not have such consequences. It is sometimes offered as an argument against divine command theory, that moral codes need to change if they are to reflect human changes. Similar arguments are offered against natural law morality. However, it is possible to form a synthesis of the two types of moral code which preserves the inviolate, objective character of the morality which the divine command theorist espouses, without losing any of its force or relevance through the changing circumstances of history. The important concepts in natural law theory which are of assistance in forming such a synthesis are the concept of human nature and that of the distinction between primary and secondary precepts of the natural law.

First consider some remarks on Aquinas's theory which have been made by two recent writers, Battaglia and O'Connor:
The term 'natural' can refer to

the notion that things in the material world have fixed 'natures' and that these are unchanging, and are normative for human beings in a moral sense. Much natural law reasoning in the past has proceeded from this assumption, and it is this association of the word 'natural' that makes the idea of natural law so open to attack today... I see no need to defend the idea of natural law against attacks upon this discarded meaning... [A] way of formulating the notion of natural law must be found that respects the historicity of human experience of the world.[22]

Like Platonic natures, natural laws have been seen as fixed and unchanging... Much like political laws they had a kind of propositional form - as commands or precepts - and seemed to allow no room for human freedom or autonomy, much less for change or history.[23]

Whatever Thomas meant in the thirteenth century, whatever his combination of the Bible, Christian Platonism and Aristotle meant in his time, it is unlikely to have much relevance to ours, except as it has been translated out of a cultural perspective far different from that of a man who lived before the scientific revolution, the European discovery of America, and the awakening of the modern sense of history.[24]

For historical reasons we are acutely and practically aware of the variability of human practice in a way in which Thomas was not.[25]

Unfortunately, the will to rationality, even allied to great philosophical acumen, is not enough to guide a man to the truth. He must also know (a) what rational argument can do and what are its limits, and (b) what evidence we can appropriately use as material for the processes of reason. The rise of natural science, mathematics, and formal logic in the past three hundred years has made both (a) and (b) clear to us. But St. Thomas has a very imperfect idea of both. We are lucky enough to have the right models for rationality; he had the bad luck to be born too early.[26]

The fall of the stone is better explained by the theory of gravitation than by the statement that stones have a natural appetite for resting-places near the centre of the earth.[27]

The progress of science is a continual refutation of the theory of essences.[28]

[Psychology and social science] confirm what common experience suggests, namely, that the goods and activities in which people find happiness are many and various.[29]

If man has a common, essential nature then there ought to be evidence of it, but

> we do not in fact find this unity of structure, capacity and behaviour among human beings any more than we do among other species... In bodily structure... men may vary indefinitely [and similarly for other human features].[30]
>
> Thomas does not tell us how we are to find which is the primary and which is the secondary end of an action.[31] ... Most of all, the difference between natural law in the *Commentum* and in the *Summa* is that in the former natural law is a matter of the *ends of actions* whereas in the latter it is a matter of the *good of man*.[32]
>
> Thomas once held a very different notion of natural law. The theory expressed in the *Commentary on the Sentences* was based on our knowledge of the natural purpose of specific human actions and Thomas did not explain how we come to know these purposes. Around the time of the writing of *de Veritate* he decided that synderesis is the power by which we come to know the precepts of the natural law.[33]
>
> If the detailed precepts of the natural law can be supposed to change... or even, less radically, if *our knowledge* of these detailed precepts changes, what becomes of the theory of natural law as an objectively based and rationally defensible basis for morality? This objectivity and rationality is, after all, its great apparent advantage. Yet it seems inevitable either that its detailed prescriptions become irrelevant and inapplicable to a society changed by education and technology or that they are accommodated to these changes. In that case, the theory is, in its application, as relativist as any other.[34]

Aquinas believed that human nature is fixed.[35] Like Aristotle he held that the distinctive feature of human beings is their rationality: this is what sets them apart from the beasts. On the other hand, he accepted that in certain respects human nature can change. One may say that human nature has both essential and accidental properties or qualities. The real thrust of many of the arguments above is that we now know certain things that Aquinas did not know, and that this knowledge refutes the claim that there is an essential nature in man, or the claim that there is one goal at which he should aim in order to achieve happiness. This refutation is taken to be an empirical matter, a consequence of science, natural and social. However, the main points expressed against Aquinas are easily rebutted, for they are based upon fundamental misconceptions concerning the meaning of 'essential', the role of science, and the relevance of history.

Man is possessed of, in fact he is partly constituted by, an immortal soul, in the view of Aquinas (and indeed of all orthodox Christians before and since). His rationality is an aspect or function of his soul. Now whether or not man really does have a soul is a metaphysical question, and one which can not in principle be answered by science. No amount of scrutiny of the body by means of any scientific instrument will reveal the presence of a soul, nor will it confirm the absence of one. Similarly, in the case of the other objects in creation, the animals, plants and the rest, the metaphysical essence is not something to be observed by scientific method. Science can presumably investigate whether, given certain criteria for rationality, any particular being meets those criteria in respect of its behaviour: this is a matter for psychology and the social sciences. But even if a being born of human parents failed to demonstrate that it possessed rationality, science could not conclude from this that the being was not human. For some human beings are, both in common sense terminology and in Thomist philosophy, irrational at times or even unable ever to act rationally. Aquinas's position is not incompatible with the existence of humans who can not act rationally, for it holds, along with common sense, that rationality is the distinctive feature of man in his best or complete state: a child, a sleeper, a madman, a moron - none of these ceases to be (or fails to become) human on account of a deficiency of rationality; they all possess, according to traditional Christianity, an immortal soul.

Far from refuting the existence of essences, there is a sense in which science actually presupposes their existence, even in its physical materialist manifestations. If we are able to group together certain beings as members of a class, if, for example, social science is to make any study of human beings, then there must be some property or quality which all these things have in common. O'Connor acknowledges that one can not without circularity define as human those beings born of human parents, but retreats into the claim that what constitutes being human is something ill defined and shadowy, a matter of degree.[36] Men vary considerably in every conceivable way and therefore there can be nothing common to them all: this is the basis of his claim. But it is clearly self refuting. In order to assert it one must assume that one has some knowledge of what it is to be a man, independently of variable attributes: 'men vary indefinitely' presupposes that something *invariable* is common to all the beings who are said to vary, namely, whatever it is that enables us to call them men despite their variations. What we have in common is not our membership of an identifiable biological taxon: rather, we are members of that taxon in virtue of what we have in common. That common feature might conceivably be a physical attribute, but in Thomist terminology it is an essence. The advantage which Thomism displays over O'Connor's brand of philosophy is clear: the former admits, discusses, and terms 'essence' whatever it is that human beings have in common; whereas the latter presupposes, but denies and refuses to name, the very same thing.

Nor should one be misled by the supposed superiority of the scientific explanation of the way things behave, compared with the Thomist account. If one

purpose, of an object can be established by reference to the intention of a designer. If there is a dispute about whether the true function of a screwdriver is to turn screws or to lever the lids off tins, then appeal can be made to the intention of the person who made the screwdriver. But science, and pure natural law, may make no reference to the intentions or purposes of natural objects or beings (*qua* objects or beings, that is; I do not mean to deny that science can ascribe intentions to people, for example, but only to assert that it can not determine what people are for, as it were). What this argument shows is not that it is irrational to distinguish between the various functions a nose may serve, selecting as the true function (or purpose, if that is not taken to imply deliberate design) smelling or breathing rather than operating digital telephones, but that such a selection is based on presuppositions about the value of smelling or breathing which go beyond the limits of pure science or pure natural law: science and natural law have as data upon which to operate only the observations of what in fact occurs in the world. When common sense judgments, such as the judgment that a nose is primarily for smelling or breathing, are made, they are made with implicit reference to the place something, in this case a nose, occupies in a larger scheme of things which includes some assignment of values. We see life as a good, so we are entitled to claim that a nose is best suited to breathing rather than to opening doors, though it may do both equally well. Nor is it relevant to the argument here that only a nose can smell: only an atomic reaction of a certain type, one might say, can wreak such havoc as was wrought at Hiroshima, but one can not on that basis claim that the true function of an atomic reaction of that type is to cause widespread destruction. (Of course, one can say that destruction is the primary purpose of an atomic bomb, but this assertion can only be justified by reference to the intention of a designer). The distinction between primary and secondary ends is one that is commonly made and is available not only to common sense but also to natural law theorists and biological scientists, provided that it is recognized that in utilizing such a distinction they step beyond the bounds of strict science or strict natural law.[40] In fact Aquinas can, with all theists, avail himself of the notion of purposive design in the features of natural objects in a way not open to an atheistic scientist, since he believes that all things were created by a purposive agent. He need not tell us how to distinguish primary from secondary ends because in general the distinction is an obvious one to those whose values coincide to any great extent with his own. And for most people, the coincidence of value is great, it seems safe to say: they see life as a good, and acknowledge as goods the various ways in which we put into operation our distinctively human faculties for the purpose of promoting or enhancing life, regardless of whether or not they share Aquinas's metaphysical presuppositions.

It can now be seen why there is no conflict between an account of our knowledge of the precepts of natural law in terms of the ends of human actions and an account of those precepts in terms of the good of man: the way in which we distinguish the ends of human actions, their true ends (whether primary or accepts Swinburne's distinction between scientific and personal explanation[37] then one can, rather, claim with some plausibility that what underpins Aquinas's account of the behaviour of the things in creation will actually lead to a better sort of explanation than anything science has to offer. For there is a sense in which scientific explanation, so called, is no real *explanation* at all, but consists in *description* of what happens rather than an account of *why* it happens. The law of gravity goes no way whatever towards explaining the fall of the stone, except for those who misunderstand it. That law describes how, in what manner, the stone falls, and amounts to no more than an embellishment, a description in other terms, of what everyone already knows, namely, that the stone falls. It does not fall *because* of the law of gravity, nor does gravity *make* it fall: it just falls, and that is a brute fact. To put the point in another way, there is, as far as can be known, nothing more to gravity over and above the measurable behaviour of the stone: the disposition of objects to move towards each other in certain circumstances just is their gravity, as it were, and is hardly explained by positing an occult force which manifests itself in no other way than that disposition itself.[38] Whether or not one agrees with Aquinas's metaphysics, one can not sensibly hold that in these circumstances the scientific 'explanation' is superior to the Thomistic one, except insofar as it allows detailed predictions to be made. Yet such predictions as can correctly be made by relying on scientific laws confer no more explanatory power on the scientific hypotheses that underlie those laws than they would have in the absence of predictive ability. And if one does indeed accept Aquinas's metaphysics then one has, at least, some grasp of the way in which motion can be considered as the effect of a purposive mind, and hence of the way in which it is liable to the personal explanation which, as Swinburne notes, is likely to be the more satisfying, the more genuinely explanatory, form of explanation.

Finally (leaving to one side some of the more extravagant claims involved - what moral principle could have been subverted by the European discovery of America?[39]) one can dispose of the notion that we have, from empirical observation, more knowledge than Aquinas could have had concerning variations in moral practice and the goals of man. There is no a priori reason why the variations in moral practice of which we are aware should not have been in evidence among Aquinas's contemporaries and forerunners. One need not be wholly reliant upon the evidence of the past seven centuries in order to conclude that such variations exist. Empirically, as a matter of observable fact, it is difficult to understand what new, morally relevant observations could have been made in recent history which could not have been made by Aquinas; and all the morally relevant information we have gained from observing human behaviour might, in fact, have been fully available to Aquinas. If recent history has brought new information to light, then this is something which needs to be demonstrated. Granted, technological innovations have allowed us to make progress in the way we conduct our affairs, giving us ever more efficient means of achieving our ends. But the difference between means used in the past and means used now does not give rise to any relevant new knowledge about variations in moral practices. Nor is the role of empirical observation any clearer where goals and means to happiness are concerned: people seek happiness in various ways, but whether or not they find it in those ways has to be shown, and if it could be shown, this would not refute the claim, which seems plausible, that those ways have a feature in common, namely, that they all involve the exercise of our distinctively human faculties. Further, if our grasp of moral truths and, especially, our reliance upon the usefulness of our rationality in assessing moral claims, is dependent upon the current state of our scientific knowledge, then *pace* O'Connor, we could never know what he claims we know, that is, that we now have the right model for the relation between rationality and morality, where Aquinas lacked it, since that claim would itself be liable to refutation by tomorrow's scientific discovery.

Aquinas describes natural law as yielding both primary and secondary precepts. Secondary precepts can change with changing circumstances, including changes in the accidental elements of human nature. If his account of the distinction is flawed or incoherent or unintelligible for any reason, or if his admission that moral precepts can change leads to moral relativism, then his account of natural law will be unacceptable, in itself or as an account of Christian morality.

Aquinas's view, which remains the view of the Catholic church, was that the primary end of sexual intercourse is procreation, while its secondary end is the strengthening of the bond of mutual affection between man and wife. The distinction between primary and secondary ends corresponds to the distinct between primary and secondary precepts: a primary precept will direct hu activity towards its primary end, while a secondary precept will steer act towards a secondary end. In some cases the distinction between primary secondary ends will be, or seem, intuitively obvious, and a matter of cor sense. A man's nose, for instance, will generally and uncontroversially be ac as being primarily for breathing and smelling. Now from the point of strict natural law, and for that matter from the point of view of a science as value free as it can be, there is no ground to distinguish one function o or one group of functions it fulfils, as being the primary function or f There is no criterion by which one can decide that smelling and breathir real or true or proper functions of a nose: its functions are constituted o uses to which it is put. So a man may argue that, because he uses h operating a digital telephone or for opening doors, these are its funct not do for the scientist to base his selection of breathing or smelling function of a nose on some account which shows that, in evoluti smelling and breathing are the functions which promote sur evolutionary terms, in the terms of biological science, survival is n rather something which simply occurs under favourable condition no aim or purpose. Where artefacts are concerned, the true f secondary) from any accidental ends they may have, is by considering their relation to the good of man. Thus synderesis, which is conscience in its most basic operation, is the faculty by which we perceive that the true end of, say, sexual intercourse is procreation rather than any of the various other uses to which it could be put. It is not simply that our observations lead us to the knowledge that sexual intercourse does in fact, often at any rate, result in offspring, but that we can see how it fits into the scheme of the good for man when it serves to procreate, in a way more obvious and compelling than the way in which it fits in with the good for man if aimed at pleasure or if perverted in some way.

The charge that changeability of the secondary precepts of the moral law leads to relativism is mistaken. Consider political laws: a law may be passed to prevent, say, the distribution of some cosmetic substance because in the current state of the manufacturing process the substance can not be made pure, and has a high likelihood of causing skin damage. After a few years have elapsed, the manufacturing process is refined to such an extent that the cosmetic can be produced wholly free from impurity, and is entirely harmless. Then the law may be changed to allow its distribution once more. Now this procedure involves no abandonment of principle or change of heart on the part of the legislators: the law was passed not with the specific intention of finishing the distribution of the cosmetic for ever, but clearly with the primary intention of preventing people from suffering skin damage. When circumstances change to the extent that the substance is harmless, no law is necessary to prevent its distribution. Exactly the same principle applies in the case of secondary moral precepts: the natural law, in conjunction with an understanding of the divine (in Aquinas's account) purpose for man, bids one refrain from harming oneself or another. In order to bring about the state of affairs enjoined by this principle, certain secondary precepts will be desirable. If in the thirteenth century it is the case that, for example, optical technology offers no way of enabling one to observe the sun for more than a brief moment without incurring serious eye damage, one may say that the secondary precept of natural law that can be derived is a precept forbidding observation of the sun. But if at a later date techniques are developed which permit the safe observation of the sun, a special filter is invented, let us suppose, then that secondary precept becomes void. A similar argument could be framed in relation to contraceptive technology, if the supposed wrongness of contraception lay in some feature of it (such as its physical intrusiveness) which had to be present in earlier forms but which later developments contrived to avoid. Nothing in any of this suggests that a path towards moral relativism is being followed.

As regards the primary precepts of the moral law, in this case the precept that one may not harm oneself or another, it is difficult to imagine what possible progress in science or historical knowledge could render them irrelevant. And the assertion that such unchangeability amounts to an infringement of human autonomy or freedom is little more than absurd: as has been argued earlier, the objective nature of moral law is no more a restriction on human action than is the objective nature of logic or of the physical world. That theft is wrong is, if a fact, a fact that in no way impinges upon my freedom to steal or my autonomous decision to steal.

This clarification and defence of natural law prepares the way for understanding how it can be combined with divine command morality. Man's nature, proper ends, and the primary precepts of natural law can be regarded as having been established by divine *fiat*. Secondary precepts, which may or may not have been made explicit in revelation, can be reasoned out in the knowledge of the divinely ordained precepts concerning the fundamentals of morality, as can a certain amount of information about correct and incorrect behaviour which can not be gained from scripture. This understanding of the relation between divine commands and natural law does justice to the claims, hard to doubt, that to a certain degree one can reason out one's duties without having any knowledge of scripture (since all men share some divinely provided means of ascertaining, in part, the divine will, namely reason and conscience) and also that Christianity must envisage the whole moral system in terms of the will of God.

Christian rationalism

But it might yet be shown that divine commands form no part of Christian morality, even if revelation is essential to it in some way. It could be argued that, although the foundation of morality is given by divine revelation, it is nevertheless quite possible to work out a system of morals which, while fundamentally religious in that it builds upon this divinely revealed foundation, need not and does not make any essential use of divine commands. The motivation for formulating and defending a moral theory of this sort may be the conviction that divine command morality offers an inadequate account of the nature, the force and the role of both reason and conscience in moral matters, together with an acceptance of the point made above, that reason and natural law are in need of revelational support. For in their nature the pronouncements of reason may have, and those of conscience invariably do have, applicability to moral decisions. Further, they may be felt as having overwhelming force, perhaps seeming to be incorrigible or self evidently true; and their function may be to guide one's actions in working through particular moral predicaments whether or not there exists any commandment, supposedly issued by God, pertaining to such predicaments. The Christian who wishes to put forward a moral system which is free from divine commands (his position can conveniently be referred to as Christian Rationalism) may also oppose his account to that of the Christian Platonist, taking that account to entail a denial of God's omnipotence. The Christian Rationalist may, then, accept that God's power ranges over everything except necessary truths, justifying this exception on the ground that the denial or modification of a necessary truth leads to incoherence, but may further claim that moral truths are not species of necessary truth; he may, that is, accept divine voluntarism. Yet while granting that God's commands could form the basis of morality, and would both define the moral status of actions and create genuine moral duties (rather than merely laying down rules which it would be prudent for creatures to adhere to) if He were actually to issue commands for that purpose, the Christian Rationalist may insist that divine commands do not in fact form the basis of morality, and that any divine commands which have been issued have a different purpose. An argument for this position may be outlined as follows.

First, divine commands are wholly superfluous to the business of establishing moral principles and making particular decisions. Once we have an understanding, even an imprecise understanding, of a few basic religious or theological premises (which need make no mention of God's commands) we are in a position to apply reason and conscience without further assistance. Whereas those moral systems which are derived from reason alone, or from conscience alone, or from a combination of these, will always prove to be inadequate to the task of demonstrating what is the proper end or purpose of mankind, and of maintaining moral objectivity, Christian Rationalism overcomes these inadequacies by building upon a divinely revealed foundation. It is, in effect, rationalist or naturalist ethics plus one important explanatory piece of information concerning the purpose of creation - information which these systems can not provide. For no amount of examination of the world, including the nature of its inhabitants, can tell us why it should be any particular way: without some outside input, so to speak, any imperatives which are supposed to apply in the world will always be hypothetical rather than categorical, and it will always be open to the selfish or the perverse or the downright wicked rationally to question the desirability of, or to deny the moral relevance of what is posited by the conditional clause of any such hypothesis.

Second, even the most cursory glance at scripture shows that many of the commands to be found there are addressed to particular people in particular circumstances, and are not meant to have general application.[41] A more thorough consideration of scripture in its historical context indicates that other commands, though more generally applicable, are best understood as intended to function only within a certain culture. Also to be found are commands of a third type, commands which can reasonably be taken as intended to apply universally, rather than being valid only for particular individuals or societies or historical periods. Examples of the first type of command are the instructions listed in Exodus concerning the dimensions of the tabernacle and curtains and the materials to be used in their construction; the dietary instructions in Leviticus and the laws in Exodus regarding slaves are examples of the second type; the ten commandments and the injunction to love one's neighbour are examples of the third type.

That it is possible to make such distinctions between types of divine command suggests that the commands in question can not form the foundation of our moral theory. For clearly commands of the first two types will not suffice, and the commands of the third type are only to be acknowledged as universally binding because they are derivable from the exercise of conscience and reason. We know that it is not morally obligatory to refrain from eating hares because eating hares offends neither conscience nor reason;[42] but we know that we ought not to steal because, once we have some insight into the proper ends of mankind, stealing is seen to be irrational (and it is generally offensive to conscience). Divine commands are therefore irrelevant to the foundation of our moral theory (in the case of those which are not universally applicable) or superfluous (in the case of those which could be derived in other ways). This is not to say that the commands of the decalogue are irrelevant to morality, but only to insist that their being divine commands does not of itself enable them to be taken as the foundation of morality upon which all else can be built. Then the ten commandments can be taken as directing our attention to, or emphasizing, moral principles which we can know to be true on other grounds.

It may be objected here that the Christian Rationalist's acceptance of divine voluntarism commits him to the further acceptance of the proposition that, whether or not the commands of the decalogue are justifiable on other grounds, the fact that God has issued them is sufficient for them to constitute an objective moral code and to be morally binding. There are two ways of meeting this objection. It can be argued that the distinction between types of divine commands shows that the fact that something is divinely commanded is not in itself sufficient to make it universally obligatory. Just as some commands are issued with the intention that they apply only in certain circumstances or to certain people, so too the commands of the decalogue are addressed not to mankind as a whole but to the Israelites under Moses. They are, then, not commanded *as the basis of morality* but for some other reason. They are not therefore binding now in virtue of being divine commands, since that is not the reason why they were issued, and are, rather, binding now only in virtue of their being the very principles that the Christian will see to be true by his use of reason and conscience. Alternatively, it could be maintained that scripture is not to be taken literally; that it is, for example, a blend of religiously interpreted history and artistic, literary, creative writing. Such a claim can not too lightly be dismissed as fatal to the very Christianity of the one who asserts it, since it is possible that the function of scripture is no more than to produce, say, a state of mind in which devotion to God is paramount: people can and do claim to be Christians while simultaneously rejecting the notion that literal truth is to be found or even sought in scripture. Then there would, quite simply, be no divine commands of the type which could form the basis of morality, for there would be no divine commands at all.

A basic revelation

What the Christian Rationalist needs to show, if he is to present an account in opposition to divine command theory, is not only how his position does greater justice to the functions in morality of reason and conscience than divine command theory does, but also how there can be a basic revelation which does not contain divine commands as an essential element but which nevertheless indicates, in sufficient detail to allow the inference of moral principles, what man's general end or purpose is. Of course, the moral principles thus inferred must accord with those of traditional theism: in particular, nothing of importance must be omitted. If the application of reason and conscience to a basic revelation were to result in a moral system in which there was no place for altruism, for example, then it could scarcely be accepted by the traditional theist as a rival either to Christian Platonism or to divine command morality.

(Further, if the basic revelation is to be scriptural then it must be shown by the Christian Rationalist who denies any literal significance to scripture exactly how such information is to be extracted from what is essentially an uninformative work, devoid of facts. This could perhaps be shown by way of a claim that scripture contains a message, but not a literal message; a claim that, for instance, a reading of scripture produces a change of heart or a particular frame of mind in the reader who is sufficiently appreciative and attentive. In any event, such a position is not obviously incoherent; nor would it be necessary to defend it in order to defend Christian Rationalism generally, since it relates only to an extreme form of Christian Rationalism according to which there are no divine commands. Alternatively, a modified account may be offered: the Bible could be taken as largely non literal but containing some factual information, such as the information that there really existed a historical Jesus who was intimately related to God and whose acts and words had a deep impact on people and events. However, in what follows I shall ignore this extreme position, having drawn attention to it only indicate the possibility that a Christian could conceivably deny the truth of divine command theory by denying the existence of divine commands).

The basic revelation that Christian Rationalism requires must therefore be: first, something other than can be derived from reason and conscience; second, free from any essential use of divine commands; third, sufficient, when combined with reason and conscience, for the inference of a moral system which is broadly in line with that of traditional Christianity; and fourth, contained in scripture (assuming what I take for granted here, namely that there is no other source of revelation that would be accepted as such by Christians).

Presumably it is uncontroversial to say that the Gospels strongly impart the message that it is a good thing to love one's neighbour. (This should not be taken as an assertion that that is the main message of the Gospels or of any part of the Bible, for that would be flatly denied by many Christians. But it is a common enough claim, and one that would be made by many people who, if not actually practising Christians, were brought up in a society whose values stem from Christianity originally - the sort of claim that is quite familiar in our own society). Suppose this to be the message that the Christian Rationalist takes as his basic revelation. There are commands, indeed, in scripture which say that one ought to love one's neighbour, but these do not enter into the account here: first, it can be maintained that these commands are not intended to be a foundation for a moral system - this point was noted above; but more importantly, what is offered as basic revelation on this account is that it is a good thing to love one's neighbour, and this is not equivalent to a command. This alone will not be enough information upon which to build a recognizably Christian moral system, but as a revelation it occurs within the context of a creator and a creation: the Christian Rationalist believes that there is a God who creates the world, that He somehow imparts a message by way of revelation, and that it is a good thing (by which he understands that it is pleasing to God) to love one's neighbour. If this basic revelation measures up to the four criteria listed above then the Christian Rationalist may reasonably claim to have a strong defence for his position. The discussion here is concerned with the third criterion, that is, with whether this basic revelation can be combined with reason and conscience to produce a moral system which is acceptable to a Christian. (It has already been argued that love of neighbour, that is, genuine altruism rather than the sort of altruism which is ultimately justified in terms of self interest, is not something that is dictated by reason; I take it to be fairly clear that conscience can not be relied upon to commend it; so the first criterion is met. That the second and fourth are also met is obvious too).

What the Christian Rationalist is maintaining can be put in this way: granted, God can will anything that is logically possible; but we do not need to rely on His commands to know what He wills, because He has given us a conscience to enable us to make moral decisions, powers of reason to enable us to apply moral decisions universally, and revelation both to let us know that we ought to apply moral decisions universally, having regard to the interests of others even when that is not dictated by reason, and also to prevent our use of conscience from leading to moral relativism. If the measure of acceptability to traditional Christians of a moral system is its ability to match the commands of the decalogue, then Christian Rationalism comes up to that measure. The ten commandments lay down duties towards God and duties towards men; the former are to be inferred from a conception of God as the Almighty creator; the latter can be inferred from His revelation, which shows that altruism is a good thing. For an Almighty God obviously deserves honour and respect: it is in the nature of man to accord these things to such a being; it would be wholly irrational to worship false Gods; and every day is to kept holy, if this means no more than that one should honour and respect God on that day. Loving one's neighbour, taken in conjunction with rational self interest and the normal dictates of conscience, will lead inevitably to those precepts which concern duties towards men.

The reply of the divine command theorist

There are three main lines of argument which the divine command theorist can pursue by way of reply to the Christian Rationalist. These are directed against three of the claims made by the latter, and can be put as follows:

1. The account offered by the Christian Rationalist suggests that he considers that divine command theory marginalizes or altogether dispenses with conscience and reason in moral matters. But obedience to God's commands, whatever they may be, is not at all incompatible with the exercise of reason and conscience. There is something to be said for the distinction made earlier between different types of divine command, but the role of conscience and reason is not merely to separate the universally binding commands from those of limited applicability on the ground that the former could be derived anyway without reference to God's commands. First, conscience and reason may play a vital (though not necessarily unaided) part in bringing about the initial belief in the existence of God and in working out what His attributes may be. Our reason and our conscience have, too, an epistemological function, in that they help us to form a judgment as to whether a command really is of divine origin. But they are not paramount, as I have argued earlier: presumably God could, in some suitably impressive way, cause us to know without doubt that He wanted us to behave in a certain manner even if such behaviour would initially be at odds with both reason and conscience; and after all, to maintain otherwise would be to make man the final arbiter in moral matters, whereas a decent humility suggests that this could not be correct. The chief motivation for denying divine command theory (given that the Christian Rationalist is also a believer in divine voluntarism) is based upon an error.

2. There are other important divine commands, besides those of the decalogue, which can not be dismissed as particular rather than universal yet which could not be inferred by applying reason and conscience to a basic revelation of the sort proposed by the Christian Rationalist. He is, then, mistaken again in supposing that the precepts of the decalogue represent all that is essential to Christian moral theory. No amount of reasoning will yield the conclusion that it is wrong to engage in sodomy or bestiality: a consideration of the way the world is will only reveal that those who engage in such practices will to that extent be unable to produce offspring.[13] One can not, on the basis of reason alone, or even on the basis of reason mixed with altruism, reach conclusions about the sole justifiable purpose of physical processes and functions: without further assistance one can conclude no more than that things are for whatever they are used for. And it seems to be an undeniable matter of fact that the consciences of some people at least do not lead them to consider that the above practices are immoral. Yet the laws prohibiting sodomy and bestiality can not easily be understood as having application only to particular people at a particular time or within a certain

cultural setting, for they seem to be directed to man *qua* man rather than *qua* Israelite or shepherd or farmer, etc.

3. It is by no means clear that the Christian Rationalist can show that his moral system will supply even those precepts contained in the decalogue. Loving one's neighbour as oneself certainly has implications for universality and consistency in moral matters, but it has few if any implications for the *content* of universally applicable moral principles.[44] Depending on my nature, loving my neighbour as myself need not preclude my making love to his wife; and many acts which would be forbidden absolutely by the precepts of the decalogue would not be forbidden by the principles derived from reason and altruism if they were committed with the consent of everyone involved. Perhaps the duties to God which are listed in the decalogue are no more than what a belief in God would entail, though this is debatable; but certainly, reason and altruism are insufficient resources from which to derive all the duties towards men, and the dictates of conscience in this respect are, being different for different people, wholly unreliable.

But how is the divine command theorist to discriminate between the precepts which forbid eating hares etc. and those which forbid sodomy and bestiality? He can not of course say that reason dictates the latter commands but not the former, for that is precisely what he denies, on the above account. Christians have dealt with such commands in various ways. There have been attempts to interpret them allegorically;[45] or they have been dismissed as no longer relevant because they are contained within the Old Testament, which has been superseded by the New - so they are no longer applicable. Either of these responses is fraught with difficulty for anyone who espouses divine voluntarism and takes scripture fairly literally. For unless one knows that such acts as eating hares are *not* wrong, one has no reason to seek or offer an allegorical interpretation in the first place (assuming, that is, that hare consumption is not a widely accepted or well known metaphor). And, crucially, the Old Testament contains the Decalogue, which no traditional theist will wish to regard as having been superseded (though he may say that it has been complemented) by anything in the New Testament.

It is quite feasible that a divine command theorist should accept the proscription of hare consumption: God has forbidden it, and that is all there is to be said about the matter. This position is not *inconsistent* with traditional Christianity, even though it might be rarely (but, perhaps, increasingly less rarely) held by traditional Christians. Alternatively, if he wishes to ignore it, he may still offer an argument to the effect that a command forbidding the consumption of hares is irrational if intended as universally binding, and that there is a good case, therefore, for considering it to be intended to have only local application. He may defend his claim, that it is irrational if taken as universally binding, on the ground that it does not cohere well with the many other divine commands which form a distinctive and consistent set, since they all appear to have something in common in their direction towards establishing certain forms of human behaviour, while the ban on eating hares does not. On the other hand, the laws forbidding sodomy and bestiality, while not rationally derivable, do seem to cohere well with that set of commands which seeks to put human society on a particular course, namely the course towards an unselfish devotion to others and to God which is characterized by, *inter alia*, a concern to place a higher value on procreation than on sexual pleasure and to ensure that one functions, not in any way one rationally can (which, provided one has regard for conscience and the need for altruism, is permissible for the Christian Rationalist), but in the way that one ought, as suggested by God's plan for mankind insofar as it has been revealed. The extent to which this attempt to distinguish binding from non binding commands will work is perhaps not great: it is dependent upon an account of what it is to be a distinctive and consistent set of commands - a case can, after all, be made for regarding *all* scriptural commands as such a set. Nevertheless, it is one possible response that may be offered by the divine command theorist; but the first response mentioned above, the acceptance of such proscriptions as binding, can be defended more strongly.

A basic revelation of the type proposed by the Christian Rationalist will therefore prove to be inadequate to the task of supporting that system of morality which is distinctively Christian. Possibly, a revelation with larger content could have the required function, but it is clear that as the proposed basic revelation becomes more detailed in content, there is (recalling that it is to be based on scripture) progressively less justification for excluding divine commands; the revelation suggested by Christian Rationalism as basic would then seem more like an *ad hoc* interpretation of scripture designed specifically to exclude divine commands. Yet such an interpretation could not have the principled defence that, say, the Christian Platonist could (though I do not say he would) offer, for unlike the latter, the Christian Rationalist sees nothing amiss in divine voluntarism, and does not reject as incoherent an account of morality according to which good is whatever God says it is. In short, any attempt to base a Christian moral system upon no more than an intuition, whether or not inspired by Christian scriptures, that love is a good thing, will fail because it lacks sufficient content. The concept of love, of God or neighbour, needs to be filled out in rather more detail than is suggested by, for example, the Golden Rule. John the Apostle suggests a way in which content is to be given to the concept of love, a way which supports the case made by the divine command theorist: 'By this we know that we love the children of God, when we love God, and keep his commandments. For this is the love of God, that we keep his commandments'[46].

There is in Christianity a tradition of interpreting scripture non literally; but apart from the problem of where to draw the line, of what may and may not be thus interpreted, there are difficulties if this is to be applied to divine commands, whether in the decalogue or in the words of Christ, as some would do.[47] It was noted earlier that wholly non literal interpretations of scripture ought not to be dismissed too lightly; but the argument above shows that, in a Christian context, some core of literal truth needs to be retained. For if we disregard the literal meaning of what has, according to the tradition, been revealed of God's will, we are at least as likely to make the teachings of scripture conform to our own will as we are to make them conform to His. To extend the procedure of interpretation from positive human law to positive divine commands risks a collapse of Christian morality and a descent into moral relativism, with nothing to distinguish the result from non Christian accounts of what it is to be moral. In fact, even a Christ-inspired concern for others would not distinguish it: other systems show the same concern. Nor need such a concern be the outcome of a personal interpretation of the Old or New Testament writings, for without some anchor, some literal reading which may not be subject to interpretation, it seems that anything whatever could be the result.

Notes

1   Many claims to this effect stem from Hume's *Treatise of Human Nature*, III (i) 1, and some from Moore's *Principia Ethica*; but see too Searle (1964), 'How to Derive *Ought* from *Is*', *Philosophical Review* 73, pp. 43-58.
2   My argument here is not to be taken as denying that values can legitimately be inferred from bare facts; it does not directly support the commonplace view. Rather, my intention is to show that the common denial of the possibility of inferring 'ought' from 'is' is not an obstacle to natural law theory, and is not strictly relevant.
3   Hart (1961), *The Concept of Law*, Oxford. See in particular chapter IX, 'Laws and Morals'.
4   Mitchell (1980), *Morality: Religious and Secular*, Oxford, p. 28.
5   The importance of this distinction has been stressed in the introduction.
6   On the pure formality of the Golden Rule, see Locke (1981), 'The Principle of Equal Interests', *Philosophical Review* 90, pp. 531-59.
7   It might be objected here that 'taken' is really the same thing as 'claimed for one's own', and would not therefore be a coherent concept if there were no longer such a category as 'belonging'. However, even if that were so it would not follow that my actions and maxim were irrational: all that follows is that my notions of stealing and of property would not be compatible with those of society at large. But I could still rationally will that my notions should be accepted by society at large. The notion of property that I use will only be inconsistent with stealing once society has in fact adopted a similar view to my own: *then* there would be no such thing as stealing, for property would in effect be held in common. For details of Kant's argument see Paton (1987), *The Moral Law*, London.

Man is possessed of, in fact he is partly constituted by, an immortal soul, in the view of Aquinas (and indeed of all orthodox Christians before and since). His rationality is an aspect or function of his soul. Now whether or not man really does have a soul is a metaphysical question, and one which can not in principle be answered by science. No amount of scrutiny of the body by means of any scientific instrument will reveal the presence of a soul, nor will it confirm the absence of one. Similarly, in the case of the other objects in creation, the animals, plants and the rest, the metaphysical essence is not something to be observed by scientific method. Science can presumably investigate whether, given certain criteria for rationality, any particular being meets those criteria in respect of its behaviour: this is a matter for psychology and the social sciences. But even if a being born of human parents failed to demonstrate that it possessed rationality, science could not conclude from this that the being was not human. For some human beings are, both in common sense terminology and in Thomist philosophy, irrational at times or even unable ever to act rationally. Aquinas's position is not incompatible with the existence of humans who can not act rationally, for it holds, along with common sense, that rationality is the distinctive feature of man in his best or complete state: a child, a sleeper, a madman, a moron - none of these ceases to be (or fails to become) human on account of a deficiency of rationality; they all possess, according to traditional Christianity, an immortal soul.

Far from refuting the existence of essences, there is a sense in which science actually presupposes their existence, even in its physical materialist manifestations. If we are able to group together certain beings as members of a class, if, for example, social science is to make any study of human beings, then there must be some property or quality which all these things have in common. O'Connor acknowledges that one can not without circularity define as human those beings born of human parents, but retreats into the claim that what constitutes being human is something ill defined and shadowy, a matter of degree.[36] Men vary considerably in every conceivable way and therefore there can be nothing common to them all: this is the basis of his claim. But it is clearly self refuting. In order to assert it one must assume that one has some knowledge of what it is to be a man, independently of variable attributes: 'men vary indefinitely' presupposes that something *invariable* is common to all the beings who are said to vary, namely, whatever it is that enables us to call them men despite their variations. What we have in common is not our membership of an identifiable biological taxon: rather, we are members of that taxon in virtue of what we have in common. That common feature might conceivably be a physical attribute, but in Thomist terminology it is an essence. The advantage which Thomism displays over O'Connor's brand of philosophy is clear: the former admits, discusses, and terms 'essence' whatever it is that human beings have in common; whereas the latter presupposes, but denies and refuses to name, the very same thing.

Nor should one be misled by the supposed superiority of the scientific explanation of the way things behave, compared with the Thomist account. If one accepts Swinburne's distinction between scientific and personal explanation[37] then one can, rather, claim with some plausibility that what underpins Aquinas's account of the behaviour of the things in creation will actually lead to a better sort of explanation than anything science has to offer. For there is a sense in which scientific explanation, so called, is no real *explanation* at all, but consists in *description* of what happens rather than an account of *why* it happens. The law of gravity goes no way whatever towards explaining the fall of the stone, except for those who misunderstand it. That law describes how, in what manner, the stone falls, and amounts to no more than an embellishment, a description in other terms, of what everyone already knows, namely, that the stone falls. It does not fall *because* of the law of gravity, nor does gravity *make* it fall: it just falls, and that is a brute fact. To put the point in another way, there is, as far as can be known, nothing more to gravity over and above the measurable behaviour of the stone: the disposition of objects to move towards each other in certain circumstances just is their gravity, as it were, and is hardly explained by positing an occult force which manifests itself in no other way than that disposition itself.[38] Whether or not one agrees with Aquinas's metaphysics, one can not sensibly hold that in these circumstances the scientific 'explanation' is superior to the Thomistic one, except insofar as it allows detailed predictions to be made. Yet such predictions as can correctly be made by relying on scientific laws confer no more explanatory power on the scientific hypotheses that underlie those laws than they would have in the absence of predictive ability. And if one does indeed accept Aquinas's metaphysics then one has, at least, some grasp of the way in which motion can be considered as the effect of a purposive mind, and hence of the way in which it is liable to the personal explanation which, as Swinburne notes, is likely to be the more satisfying, the more genuinely explanatory, form of explanation.

Finally (leaving to one side some of the more extravagant claims involved - what moral principle could have been subverted by the European discovery of America?[39]) one can dispose of the notion that we have, from empirical observation, more knowledge than Aquinas could have had concerning variations in moral practice and the goals of man. There is no a priori reason why the variations in moral practice of which we are aware should not have been in evidence among Aquinas's contemporaries and forerunners. One need not be wholly reliant upon the evidence of the past seven centuries in order to conclude that such variations exist. Empirically, as a matter of observable fact, it is difficult to understand what new, morally relevant observations could have been made in recent history which could not have been made by Aquinas; and all the morally relevant information we have gained from observing human behaviour might, in fact, have been fully available to Aquinas. If recent history has brought new information to light, then this is something which needs to be demonstrated. Granted, technological innovations have allowed us to make progress in the way we conduct our affairs, giving us ever more efficient means of achieving our ends.

But the difference between means used in the past and means used now does not give rise to any relevant new knowledge about variations in moral practices. Nor is the role of empirical observation any clearer where goals and means to happiness are concerned: people seek happiness in various ways, but whether or not they find it in those ways has to be shown, and if it could be shown, this would not refute the claim, which seems plausible, that those ways have a feature in common, namely, that they all involve the exercise of our distinctively human faculties. Further, if our grasp of moral truths and, especially, our reliance upon the usefulness of our rationality in assessing moral claims, is dependent upon the current state of our scientific knowledge, then *pace* O'Connor, we could never know what he claims we know, that is, that we now have the right model for the relation between rationality and morality, where Aquinas lacked it, since that claim would itself be liable to refutation by tomorrow's scientific discovery.

Aquinas describes natural law as yielding both primary and secondary precepts. Secondary precepts can change with changing circumstances, including changes in the accidental elements of human nature. If his account of the distinction is flawed or incoherent or unintelligible for any reason, or if his admission that moral precepts can change leads to moral relativism, then his account of natural law will be unacceptable, in itself or as an account of Christian morality.

Aquinas's view, which remains the view of the Catholic church, was that the primary end of sexual intercourse is procreation, while its secondary end is the strengthening of the bond of mutual affection between man and wife. This distinction between primary and secondary ends corresponds to the distinction between primary and secondary precepts: a primary precept will direct human activity towards its primary end, while a secondary precept will steer actions towards a secondary end. In some cases the distinction between primary and secondary ends will be, or seem, intuitively obvious, and a matter of common sense. A man's nose, for instance, will generally and uncontroversially be accepted as being primarily for breathing and smelling. Now from the point of view of strict natural law, and for that matter from the point of view of a science which is as value free as it can be, there is no ground to distinguish one function of a nose, or one group of functions it fulfils, as being the primary function or functions. There is no criterion by which one can decide that smelling and breathing are the real or true or proper functions of a nose: its functions are constituted only by the uses to which it is put. So a man may argue that, because he uses his nose for operating a digital telephone or for opening doors, these are its functions. It will not do for the scientist to base his selection of breathing or smelling as the true function of a nose on some account which shows that, in evolutionary terms, smelling and breathing are the functions which promote survival. For in evolutionary terms, in the terms of biological science, survival is not a good, but rather something which simply occurs under favourable conditions: evolution has no aim or purpose. Where artefacts are concerned, the true function, or the purpose, of an object can be established by reference to the intention of a designer. If there is a dispute about whether the true function of a screwdriver is to turn screws or to lever the lids off tins, then appeal can be made to the intention of the person who made the screwdriver. But science, and pure natural law, may make no reference to the intentions or purposes of natural objects or beings (*qua* objects or beings, that is; I do not mean to deny that science can ascribe intentions to people, for example, but only to assert that it can not determine what people are for, as it were). What this argument shows is not that it is irrational to distinguish between the various functions a nose may serve, selecting as the true function (or purpose, if that is not taken to imply deliberate design) smelling or breathing rather than operating digital telephones, but that such a selection is based on presuppositions about the value of smelling or breathing which go beyond the limits of pure science or pure natural law: science and natural law have as data upon which to operate only the observations of what in fact occurs in the world. When common sense judgments, such as the judgment that a nose is primarily for smelling or breathing, are made, they are made with implicit reference to the place something, in this case a nose, occupies in a larger scheme of things which includes some assignment of values. We see life as a good, so we are entitled to claim that a nose is best suited to breathing rather than to opening doors, though it may do both equally well. Nor is it relevant to the argument here that only a nose can smell: only an atomic reaction of a certain type, one might say, can wreak such havoc as was wrought at Hiroshima, but one can not on that basis claim that the true function of an atomic reaction of that type is to cause widespread destruction. (Of course, one can say that destruction is the primary purpose of an atomic bomb, but this assertion can only be justified by reference to the intention of a designer). The distinction between primary and secondary ends is one that is commonly made and is available not only to common sense but also to natural law theorists and biological scientists, provided that it is recognized that in utilizing such a distinction they step beyond the bounds of strict science or strict natural law.[40] In fact Aquinas can, with all theists, avail himself of the notion of purposive design in the features of natural objects in a way not open to an atheistic scientist, since he believes that all things were created by a purposive agent. He need not tell us how to distinguish primary from secondary ends because in general the distinction is an obvious one to those whose values coincide to any great extent with his own. And for most people, the coincidence of value is great, it seems safe to say: they see life as a good, and acknowledge as goods the various ways in which we put into operation our distinctively human faculties for the purpose of promoting or enhancing life, regardless of whether or not they share Aquinas's metaphysical presuppositions.

It can now be seen why there is no conflict between an account of our knowledge of the precepts of natural law in terms of the ends of human actions and an account of those precepts in terms of the good of man: the way in which we distinguish the ends of human actions, their true ends (whether primary or

8   The point, that Aquinas's natural theology is not concerned with justifying beliefs but with the search for happiness, is made by Wolterstorff. See 'The Migration of Theistic Arguments: From Natural Theology to Evidentialist Apologetics', in Audi and Wainwright (1986), *Rationality, Religious Belief, and Moral Commitment*, Cornell, pp. 38-81.

9   Aquinas, *Summa Theologiae*, IIa IIae, 154.2; *Summa Contra Gentiles*, 3, 124.

10   Rickaby (1892), *Moral Philosophy*, London, pp. 270-4.

11   See Donagan (1977), *The Theory of Morality*, Chicago, p. 103, where he argues that a communal arrangement of this sort would not result in any disadvantage to its children.

12   Copleston (1986), *Aquinas*, Penguin Books: London, pp. 231-2.

13   Farrell (1939), *A Companion to the Summa*, London, p. 76.

14   Battaglia (1981), *Toward a Reformulation of Natural Law*, New York, p. 28.

15   Aquinas, *Summa Theologiae*, Ia IIae, 91.4.

16   Copleston, op. cit., pp. 200-5.

17   That God does not *have to* will as He does in respect of our duties, and our ends in an after life, and that we therefore require information about His will rather than, simply, facts about the after life, is to be shown in the following chapters.

18   Butler (1900), *The Analogy of Religion*, London, p. 137. See also Berkeley (1955), 'On The Will of God', in *Works*, vol. 7, London.

19   Chesterton (1933), *St. Thomas Aquinas*, London, p. 37.

20   Chesterton, op. cit., p. 101.

21   MacDonald argues, citing Aquinas, that what is basic to Christian morality is not divine commands but divine reason. He says that for Aquinas 'an act is not made morally right by its having been commanded by God; it is morally right, and the law which commands it is morally good, in virtue of its being in accordance with reason'. But, 'According to Aquinas, divine reason is the sufficient and sole criterion of morally right action; human reason shares incompletely in divine reason and so is neither the sufficient nor the sole criterion of morally right action' - MacDonald (1990), 'Egoistic Rationalism: Aquinas's Basis for Christian Morality', in Beaty, *Christian Theism and the Problems of Philosophy*, University of Notre Dame Press, pp. 327-8 and 342. I discuss the relation between God's commands and His reason later, and argue that the fundamentality of divine commands can not be dismissed in the way MacDonald suggests.

22   Battaglia, op. cit., pp. 12-13.

23   Battaglia, op. cit., p. 13.

24	Battaglia, op. cit., pp. 26-7.
25	Battaglia, op. cit., pp. 51-2.
26	O'Connor (1967), *Aquinas and Natural Law*, London, p. 6.
27	O'Connor, op. cit., p. 15.
28	O'Connor, op. cit., p. 16.
29	O'Connor, op. cit., p. 27-8.
30	O'Connor, op. cit., p. 30.
31	Battaglia, op. cit., p. 55.
32	Battaglia, op. cit., p. 57.
33	Battaglia, op. cit., p. 49.
34	O'Connor, op. cit., p. 79.
35	See Nelson (1992), *The Priority of Prudence: Virtue and Natural Law in Thomas Aquinas and The Implications for Modern Ethics*, Pennsylvania State University Press: Pennsylvania, p. 33: 'Thomas... affirms that humans have a distinct *telos*, a specific end, purpose, or final good, the achievement of which constitutes their happiness... This view presumes that there is a distinct human nature. Humans, like every other creature, or thing, have a nature with a particular end or *telos*'.
36	O'Connor, op. cit., p. 30.
37	Swinburne (1979), *The Existence of God*, Oxford, chapters 2-4.
38	Cf. Leibniz's remarks in his correspondence with Clarke; in Parkinson (1988), *Leibniz: Philosophical Writings*, Dent and Sons: London, p. 228.
39	Finding people in America might conceivably alter a Biblical fundamentalist's view of man's descent from Adam, for example, or lead him to question the natives' place in relation to God's covenant with man. One could devise plausible arguments to show that the discovery might alter particular practices, but it is difficult to see that it could affect moral principles.
40	Much has been written on the relation of science, and of natural law and reason, to ultimate ends and values. For examples see: Nielsen (1985), who argues that no conclusion about what we ought to seek follows from what we do seek (*Philosophy and Atheism*, New York, pp. 165-6); Poole (1991), who says that modern science implies no objective values (*Morality and Modernity*, London, p. 67); Pirsig (1991), who claims that the idea of a value free science is a nonsense (*Lila: An Inquiry Into Morals*, London, p. 304); Wilson (1970), who sees questions of ultimate goals and values as being outside the area of formal rationality (*Rationality*, Oxford, p. xvii); Attfield (1978), who says that scientists such as Bacon and Descartes did not deny final causes but considered that, since God's purposes were hard or impossible to know, they were best left out of scientific enquiry (*God and the Secular*, Cardiff, p. 37); and Simon (1967), who argues that science is thoroughly teleological:

'With all our mechanistic good will, a chemical remains a thing ready to bring about definite effects under definite circumstances. Do you recognize a discreet expression of finality in this notion of readiness? This is how we keep arguing about teleology', (*The Tradition of Natural Law*, New York, p. 48).

41   Hobbes denied the existence in scripture of *any* universally binding divine precept, arguing that God speaks to particular people, saying different things to different men (*Leviathan*, 2, 31). This is incompatible with traditional Christianity.

42   Thus may the case be put. There is, of course, an argument to the contrary: eating hares is offensive, in reason and in conscience, to some people. I use this example, however, because it concerns a scriptural injunction that few adherents of mainstream Christian religions regard as binding.

43   I assume here that these practices can not be shown to have adverse consequences for physical or mental health.

44   Cf. Brunner (1961), *The Divine Imperative*, Lutterworth Press: London, p. 117: 'The Good is simply what *God* wills that we should do, not that which we would do on the basis of a principle of love'; and Henry (1957), *Christian Personal Ethics*, Grand Rapids, Michigan: 'The good in Hebrew-Christian theistic ethics is not that which is adapted to human nature, but it is that to which the Creator obliges human nature'.

45   For example, see the Epistle of Barnabas. This is included in Radice (1968), *Early Christian Writings*, Penguin Books: London.

46   1 John 5:2-3.

47   See Hamel (1964), *Loi Naturelle et Loi du Christ*, chapter 3, 'La Vertu d'Epikie', Desclee de Brouwer: Paris. *Epikeia*, the interpretation of (human) positive law in a manner that is contrary to the letter but judged to be in accordance with the intention of the legislator, has been considered a virtue. For examples of the extension of this form of interpretation to cover God's commands, see Mayes (1991), 'The Decalogue of Moses. An Enduring Ethical Programme?', in Freyne, S. (1991), *Ethics and The Christian*, Columba Press: Dublin, p. 27: 'The decalogue is a point of arrival, a breakthrough to what is generally valid, it emerged as a statement of meaning and intent which was to be to a limited extent fluid and changeable in itself, but which certainly always had to be interpreted for changing religious and historical situations'. In the same volume Freyne argues (in 'The Ethic of Jesus: The Sermon on The Mount Then and Now', p. 44) that Christ's words have already been interpreted for us via scripture, and that we should be aware that He did not teach timeless and unchanging moral truths. See also Mahoney (1989), *The Making of Moral Theology*, Clarendon Press: Oxford,

p. 241, where he argues that natural and divine law admit in principle of the use of *epikeia*.

5 Christian Platonism and God's nature

Introduction

My aim in this chapter is to show that there is no logical obstacle to the entailment of divine command theory that God can alter the moral status of actions. I intend to show too that His ability to do this is consistent with His traditionally accepted attributes of being good, loving, perfect and Trinitarian, each of which has been held to be inconsistent with voluntarism. The arguments I consider and oppose come principally from Christian Platonism and from those who otherwise stress God's nature as against His will and power. I begin by examining some of the particular points made by Ralph Cudworth in support of his (broadly) Platonist stance, and continue with a discussion of some more widely used arguments. I make use of some of the ideas developed earlier, to the effect that a more thorough appreciation of the teleological aspects of the creation, but including here not just the actions of creatures but creatures themselves, and their being and goodness (that is, things as well as deeds), prepares the way for a stronger defence of voluntarism than may at first seem possible. It is worth stressing that I do not here set out primarily to show that divine voluntarism actually is the basis of Christian morality, but only that it logically could be, and that its opponents themselves face serious difficulties in giving an account which does justice to the power and will of God. Still, my argument will if successful result in a *prima facie* case in favour of divine command morality as the best option among those considered.

For it is sometimes strongly argued against divine command theory that if it were correct, God could make any action good or bad, right or wrong, merely by willing it so. This is not of course a complete argument, since it is something that the divine command theorist need have no difficulty in accepting. What it needs to complete it is the addition of one of the following claims:

1. The moral status of an action can not be changed by an act of will.
2. The traditional concept of God does not allow even for the possibility of divine revision of the moral status of an action.

When the complete argument incorporates the first claim it amounts to a denial of the coherence of divine command theory, a demonstration that the theory can not possibly be correct. When the second claim is made, the argument does not deny the possibility that morality is based on divine commands but presents a challenge to the Christian to explain how divine command theory is compatible with other of his beliefs.

Cudworth and Christian Platonism

Cudworth[1] offers an argument of the first sort, though some of his points also support the second claim. What he says is this:

> moral good and evil, just and unjust, honest and dishonest (if they be not mere names without any signification, or names for nothing else, but willed and commanded, but have a reality in respect of the persons obliged to do and avoid them) cannot possibly be arbitrary things, made by will without nature; because it is universally true, that things are what they are, not by will but by nature.

There are, then, three possibilities: either the moral status of an action is just a matter of terminology, or it results from being willed and commanded (or forbidden, presumably, in the case of a bad action), or it is inherent in the nature of the action; but if morality is to be objective, and the moral status of an action is to be the ground of a genuine obligation, then it is the third possibility that must, he says, be accepted as the right one. It can be agreed without further discussion that the first possibility can be ruled out, but the following argument will show that Cudworth's claims that 'every thing is what it is by nature, and not by will' and that 'no positive commands whatsoever do make any thing morally good and evil, just and unjust, which nature had not made such before', are both false.

Much of Cudworth's argument is taken up in showing, in a reasonably convincing way, that essential natures can not be altered by acts of will. But Cudworth's opponents can accept his argument that, as far as the essential nature of a thing is concerned, God can not alter that thing, and can only exercise His power and will in either bringing it into existence or not, as He pleases. To demonstrate that essential natures can not be altered by acts of will is not at all the same thing as to demonstrate that 'every thing is what it is by nature, and not by will'. What the divine command theorist can insist upon is that the moral status of an action is not part of its essential nature. One can grant Cudworth's point that God can not make a triangle without the properties that it has by nature, for, as he notes, to do so would be contradictory: a triangle without its essential properties would not be a triangle. (It should be noted that the argument is not merely a disagreement about the meanings of words: that a triangle has three angles by definition is not to the point; what is to the point is that any plane figure which has three angles will also have three sides, and its angles will always equal in total the angle formed by a straight line). But to use the same argument for things which are good or just is to beg the question. For what is being asserted by Cudworth's opponents is that good things are not good by nature, but are good because they are pleasing to God, or commanded by God, or because they conform to His will.

One can therefore agree with Cudworth that some things have essential properties which can not be altered by divine will, on pain of contradiction. But if, as Scotus or Ockham would have it, an action is good only in virtue of conforming to God's will, then its goodness is not an essential property, but a quality which could be lacking: even though some action was generally good, it would lack the quality of goodness if it were done in defiance of a divine command that it should no longer be done, or that it should not be done on a particular occasion, or by a particular person.[2] Cudworth would need to show, in order to use his argument about essential natures effectively, that it applied universally, to the nature of all things. But if this were the case then it could be maintained that his argument would not leave room for God even to exercise His will in creation. For although Cudworth insists that 'the will and power of God have an absolute, infinite and unlimited command upon the existences of all created things to make them to be, or not to be at pleasure', one can plausibly claim that part of a full description of any created thing is, just, that it exists, as opposed to being imaginary, or a mere possibility. But then its existence would have to be included, it seems, among those essential attributes which are not, according to Cudworth, subject to being modified by a will. Moreover, even if existence is considered to be a special case, not correctly to be counted as one of a thing's attributes or qualities, Cudworth's argument goes too far. For consider what its consequences would be:

Either it is the case that a thing's nature includes the possibility of its changing, or it is not the case. If the former, then a thing can gain new attributes or lose old attributes without its nature changing; but then it could gain or lose the attributes of moral goodness or badness and yet remain the same thing. So Cudworth must take the latter option to be true. But in that case, nothing can ever change, except by coming into or going out of existence. Yet things apparently do change, all the time and in all sorts of ways. So the explanation for this must lie, for Cudworth, in God's creative activity: when I appear to get older, what must really be happening is that God is constantly creating and destroying a succession of beings who are broadly similar but who have slight differences.[3] Apart from being highly counter intuitive (and not, it should be noted, the same thing as the notion, perfectly acceptable to the traditional theist, that God constantly sustains His creatures in every moment of their being - what has been called 'continuous creation'[4]), this account has consequences which are unacceptable for moral reasons. For if there is no connecting thread of personal identity which runs through my life in such a way that I can sensibly be said to be the same person now that I was some time ago then it will be impossible to give a coherent account of moral responsibility.

One could perhaps lend support to Cudworth's position by arguing that a thing's essential nature is constituted by some, but not all, of its attributes, and that its goodness or badness is one of those attributes which can not be altered. It does indeed seem likely that talk of the essential nature of a thing is not intended to refer to each and every quality which that thing possesses: the number of hairs on a person's head, or the age of a person, are not qualities which are included in the very concept of the identity of a person.[5] Yet there is no reason to include the moral status of an action among the qualities which are essential to that action, unless the action is described in such a way that what is being referred to is not the action *per se*, but the action in a wider context. This wider context might include the motivation for the action, or its consequences, or - to press the divine command theorist's case - its relation to the divine will. When appeal is made to Aristotle,[6] who says that some things are evil as soon as named, it should be borne in mind that this is true only because such actions as murder, theft and adultery are named in such a way that implicit reference is made to their circumstances (as Aristotle's own account can be taken to confirm). What is named here is killing someone, or taking away someone's property, or having sexual intercourse with someone, none of which is in itself necessarily wrong, in circumstances which make these things wrong; circumstances which might include, for instance, acting with an inappropriate end in view. In short, if murder is wrong by nature, and unchangeably so, this is because murder means wrongful killing, and it is an analytic truth that wrongful killing is wrong; but it is not an analytic truth that there is such a thing as wrongful killing. There seems to be no ground for insisting that badness is inherent in the nature of killing in the same way that three sidedness is inherent in the nature of triangularity, unless, as is not the case, badness is logically inseparable from killing. If circumstances are crucial[7] in determining whether an action or state of affairs is morally good or bad, right or wrong, then one can more plausibly agree with Aquinas[8] that 'only God is perfect and good by nature. The goodness of created things is something added to their nature'. One need not then agree with Cudworth that all things are what they are by nature, if this is taken to mean that they must have all the qualities which they in fact have, or that goodness or badness is a quality inseparable from whatever it is that is good or bad.

But perhaps Cudworth's main point is that the moral status of an action must be part of its essential nature because if it were dependent only upon that action's being commanded (in the case of a good action) then there would be no obligation on anyone to perform it: merely having been commanded does not make an action obligatory. To argue, like those referred to by Plato's Athenian,[9] that 'legislation is never a natural process but is based on technique, and its enactments are quite artificial', is to ignore the obvious fact that what a commander bids is not made obligatory solely in virtue of having been bidden: if it really is obligatory then it will be so whether or not it is commanded by anyone, or else its obligatoriness arises from some prior obligation, grounded in natural justice, to obey that commander.

Cudworth next considers the objection that some things at least can have their moral status determined by being commanded; for where divine positive law is concerned, it is surely the case that what is otherwise morally neutral can be made obligatory when it is commanded by God: 'if all good and evil, just and unjust be not the creatures of mere will (as many assert) yet at least positive things must needs owe all their morality, their good and evil to mere will without nature'. But this is false, he says. For positive law's commands only become obligatory when the one who issues the commands has the right to do so, and this right is grounded in natural justice: we are only bound to obey if it is right, independently of being commanded to obey, that we should obey. So if God commands us to do what is otherwise morally neutral, then what is in fact obligatory and has moral goodness is not so much the action commanded as the obedience due to our rightful superior. This obedience is due in the nature of things, independently of whether or not God wills it. However, one of the reasons why this line of argument seems persuasive is that it clearly holds good where earthly commanders are concerned, for what they command could be wrong: presumably no one would accept that anything that was commanded by the state, say, was for that and no other reason right. Indeed, as is noted by Muirhead, Cudworth's arguments are better appreciated when seen in their wider context as a reaction against the ethical and social theory of Hobbes, whose elevation of will in human affairs was to be rejected, along with any contractual theory of justice which ignored the fact that covenants would not oblige unless there were, in the first place, obligations grounded in natural justice.[10]

But according to divine command theory, where God is concerned the situation is different. If it is a logical impossibility that God should command what is wrong (for right just is, on this account, conformity with the divine will), then the chief reason why Cudworth's argument is persuasive - that is, that in normal circumstances a commander could issue a wrongful command - will no longer apply. Further, the reason he actually gives for accepting that God's will can not affect the moral status even of what is commanded by positive law is that the goodness of a thing is part of its nature; but this, as has been argued above, has not been shown, and should be rejected.

In any case it is difficult to see how, on Cudworth's account (though not on the divine command theorist's account - for him, 'right' is, just, obedience to God), anyone, God included, could possess rightful authority by nature. The fact that

God is the creator may give Him authority of a sort, but it does not suffice to show how that authority is by nature rightful. And if the possession of rightful authority is simply a matter of commanding what is by its nature the right thing, then anyone will possess it insofar as he commands correctly, in which case the notion of authority, and of obedience due in virtue of the nature of the relationship between the commander and the one who is commanded, will be superfluous. It can be concluded that, if it is not the case that goodness is inherent in the nature of actions, and that if the moral status of actions is by itself a sufficient basis on which to ground their nature as either obligatory or to be avoided, then God's willing that an action be done could be sufficient to create an obligation that His creatures should do it, in just the same way that there would be an obligation if Cudworth's account were correct, and goodness were part of the unchangeable nature of good things.

Still, what sort of principle of goodness will the Christian Platonist wish to defend as fundamental to his account? Perhaps he would make one of the following claims:

1. There exists an eternal principle of goodness, something like a platonic form of the good, for instance. This is uncreated and distinct from God. Anything that has moral status, anything which from a moral standpoint is good, bad, right, wrong, permissible, etc., has its moral status in virtue of its relation to this principle. The principle is, moreover, immutable: it can not be altered even by God.

2. There is a principle of goodness which functions in the same way as in 1 and is eternal, uncreated and immutable, but which is not something distinct from God. Rather, it has its source in the very nature of God.

One could accept either of these claims as a correct account of the manner in which morality was ultimately to be explained while remaining true to at least part of what traditional theism has to say about God's relation to goodness (such as, that God is perfectly good or that He is goodness; that all good things come from Him; that whatever conforms to His will is good, and so forth). If God's will is always in accordance with the principle of goodness, and if every other thing which is good is created by Him, then there is as yet no conflict between what Christianity has to say about God's goodness and either of the two positions just outlined. However, in the theistic tradition God is the omnipotent creator of everything which exists apart from Himself. Clearly this is inconsistent with the existence of any uncreated principle which exists apart from God. So the Christian Platonist will wish to adopt some position such as 2 above.

But the question then arises whether there is any restriction on the form which the principle of goodness can take, or on what it can ordain, immutably, as good. If there is some restriction, other than one due to purely logical considerations, such that, for example, it could not be the case that torture undertaken for pleasure should ever be good, then it seems that what is now being described does not differ in any important way from position 1. For what is being suggested is that

the basis of morality lies in the nature of God in such a way that it is not dependent upon the will of God. Yet in the absence of any external constraint it ought to be the case that this aspect of His nature can take any logically possible form, with the result that there can be no reason to insist that the principle of goodness which has its source in the divine nature could never sanction torture that was undertaken for pleasure: nothing can be ruled out as necessarily bad.

But if the Christian Platonist allows that there can be no restriction upon the principle then he must concede that divine command theory is a possibility, for the principle could be just this: that anything done in accordance with a divine command is right. If he is to escape this dilemma then it seems that he must allow restrictions upon the sort of thing the principle could be, while insisting that these restrictions are not external to God. Yet if divine will can not be the source of any restrictions here, as must surely be maintained if one is to avoid conceding too much to the divine command theorist (that is, if one is to avoid saying that the nature of goodness is after all dependent upon God's will), then it is difficult to see what such a source could be.

The discussion thus far suggests a line of defence which is available to the divine command moralist who is confronted by any argument which relies upon eternal and immutable moral principles: he may pose a slightly different version of the *Euthyphro* dilemma, asking whether the immutable moral principle prescribes what it does because that thing is good, or whether on the contrary what is good is good because it is prescribed by the eternal moral law. If the Christian Platonist opts for the former alternative then he becomes involved in an infinite regress; the latter alternative would commit him to conceding that the content of the moral law was a matter of chance (or incomprehensible mystery). The worst charge which the divine command theorist has to face is that goods are, on his account, arbitrary. Even if that charge is correct, it surely describes a state of affairs which is intuitively more acceptable than one where goods are random, where what is right or wrong is a matter of chance. For we can make sense of an account according to which things are, for no apparent reason, pleasing or displeasing to God - that account, what might be thought of as a form of divine emotivism, does not differ greatly from what obtains where our own likes and dislikes are concerned. But no sense at all can be made of an account of goodness which has it that goods are good by chance - indeed, that amounts to little more than an admission that there is no sensible account to be given.

The essential problem for the Christian Platonist is to give an account of how there can be necessary moral truths, for the essence of his claim is not that moral truths can not be changed but that they could not have been other than they are. It should not be thought that such propositions as that murder is wrong, where murder is defined as wrongful killing, constitute necessary moral truths: that wrongful killing is wrong is no more a necessary *moral* truth than it is a necessary *geometric* truth that a triangle has three angles. These are merely truths of language, and are not strictly about morals or geometry at all. Nor should it be thought that God's nature as timelessly eternal provides a ground for speaking of necessary moral truths. Granted, if God is immutable, which is an entailment of (or perhaps equivalent to) His being timelessly eternal, then He can not alter any moral truth which emanates from Him. But this makes such a truth immutable rather than necessary: it can never be altered but could presumably have been other than it now is from all eternity.[11] Further, it is possible that God should eternally ordain temporally indexed moral truths, so that an immutable principle would nevertheless sanction certain behaviour at one time while prohibiting it at another.[12]

If the necessity in question is logical necessity then there seems to be no reason to admit the existence of necessary moral truth in any form, since there is no moral truth the denial of which constitutes a contradiction (with the exception, possibly, of a divine voluntarist account of moral truth according to which goodness just is, logically, conformity with the will of God; but that of course is not the sort of necessary moral truth that the Christian Platonist wants to defend). And if the necessity involved is no more than some form of physical necessity, however that could be accounted for, then it would not, one may safely suppose, constrain an omnipotent God.

Swinburne says that 'a necessary moral truth is one which holds however the world is in contingent respects', having in mind propositions such as that it is wrong to torture innocent children for fun.[13] One can question whether this conception of necessity fully captures what is usually intended in talk of the necessary in moral matters: as noted earlier, it is one thing for it always to be true, whatever the circumstances, that something is right (or wrong), but quite another for it to have to be true. To be sure, a necessary moral truth, if there is such a thing, is one that is true in all possible worlds; that is so of any species of necessary truth. But it will not do as an explanation of necessity, for it merely points out the obvious. In order to know that a world W is a possible world we need to know that everything in it is possible, that it contains no contradictions (in which case it would be an impossible world). If W is a world in which triangles have four sides then it is not a possible world; but if torture is right in W then we can not conclude that it is an impossible world, not unless we can know that torture can never be permissible; and this can not be known as a matter of logic. Knowledge of what possible worlds there may be depends upon knowledge of necessary truths, and we can only know a truth to be necessary when its denial is, or entails, a contradiction. There are indeed conceptions of the necessary other than the logically necessary, but whatever they amount to, anything which is necessarily impossible in other than the logical sense remains a logical possibility. Unless so called necessary moral truths are logically necessary (which, as noted above, they are not, since there is nothing contradictory in their denial) they remain logically possible; and this is the essence of the divine command moralist's case. It could be an eternal but contingent moral fact that rape is wrong; but if this is so, it goes no way towards demonstrating that it is a necessary moral truth that rape is wrong. If the Christian Platonist wants to defend an account according to which not even God could change the moral status of an action then he will have to do more than show that there are actions which always were, are, and will be right (or wrong), since this is insufficient to show that they must always be right (or wrong). It is certainly possible to imagine circumstances in which it is not obviously wrong to torture innocent children for pleasure.[14] These circumstances need not, of course, be likely to occur, or plausible, or even physically possible: all that is necessary to counter a claim of the sort made by Swinburne is to show that it is logically possible that there be circumstances in which it could be acceptable to torture innocent children for pleasure.

The insistence that a particular moral truth could not but be true in any possible world, even though its denial would not be contradictory, is grounded, it seems, in an inadequate appreciation of the possibilities, a lack of thoroughness in assessing what possible worlds there may be.

There are other considerations which tell against the position of the Christian Platonist, considerations which arise not from the logic of his account but rather from within the Christian tradition itself. The first of these is that God has, according to that tradition, commanded the killing of the innocent, and other actions usually taken to be immoral in the normal course of things - that is to say, they would be considered immoral by any traditional Christian if they were done without having been commanded by God.[15] The Christian Platonist can not consistently follow Kierkegaard in describing such divine interventions as the 'teleological suspension of the ethical', for suspending the ethical is precisely what is beyond God's power, on his account.[16] Unless he is to treat scripture here as a figurative rather than a literal account of God's actions,[17] then what he must argue, if he is to preserve God's goodness, along with the traditional notion that one may not do evil in order that good may come of it, is that killing the innocent is not among those things which are eternally and immutably forbidden by the principle of goodness. But then it is difficult to see how anything could be thus prohibited, if not such killing. For presumably the motivation, in part at least, for the Christian Platonist's adoption of a principle of goodness which ordains what is right and wrong unalterably (his primary concern, it is fair to say, is not with defending classical Platonism but with the specifically Christian aspects of God and morality) is his conviction that some things are so utterly and obviously bad (or good) that they could never be otherwise. Yet one would be hard put to discover a more likely candidate for unalterable badness than the killing of an innocent child.

The second consideration arising from the Christian tradition is that God is, in scriptural descriptions, very different from man: His ways are not our ways, His mind is unfathomable.[18] But in certain important respects the Christian Platonist's account of the ways of God presents Him as little more than a good and powerful person, albeit one who is always good, and very powerful. For on his account all God's actions, inasmuch as they relate to the area of morality, are explicable: God does X or commands Y because X and Y are good; He does not do Z because Z is bad.

God's nature: love, goodness, perfection, Trinity

If it is at least logically possible that God can make an action or class of actions good or bad merely by willing it so, it may still be objected that a God who could command what is currently forbidden, who could make right what is now wrong, or vice versa, could not have the character which the traditional theist ascribes to Him. That is, He could not be loving, faithful, merciful and so forth, since He might well will to treat us in a manner which was incompatible with these attributes.

Leaving to one side for the present the question whether it is plausible in a Christian context, that is to say whether it could be shown to the satisfaction of a traditional Christian who is convinced of God's loving character, that God might order His creatures to do what is currently wrong (this issue will be taken up again later), and bearing in mind the earlier argument concerning the proper ends of actions, this objection will now be considered.

The objector may hold that a God who could command torture, let us say, could not be the loving God of Christianity, whether or not He actually did command it. This is not to argue that a God who could *do wrong* would not be the sort of being that He is traditionally taken to be; for He would not in fact do wrong, whatever He might happen to do. Rather, it is to argue that being loving is incompatible with commanding or instigating torture, or even with being able to do these things. Since there would be no moral reason why God should avoid instigating torture it makes no difference whether He does so, or merely can do so: the point is that a loving God could not, it is felt, make such activity right. The divine command theorist should admit here that it is indeed inconsistent with his position that there should be a God who is loving in the sense that He will permit His creatures to suffer no hurt or distress. If that is what it is to be a loving God then the existence of such a being can be ruled out immediately by considering the pain and suffering which occurs in the world.

One proposal for solving the problem of evil is to suggest that God permits, and hence in some sense ordains, the existence of pain and suffering because it is for our long term benefit that we experience such things. Similarly, it could be argued that God could make torture right and still be a loving God if to undergo torture were better in terms of character building or soul making than not to undergo it. But this response evades the challenge made by the opponent of divine command theory: what is being offered is an account of how what seems to be opposed to our best interests could turn out not to be opposed to them, of how the avoidance of torture might turn out to be to our detriment after all. Now it is implicit in this account that it is necessarily a good thing to have one's character 'built' or one's soul 'made'; but there seems to be no reason why God could not make things otherwise.[19] Why, for instance, could not God make us in order to inflict pain upon us and ultimately to destroy us, or to leave us in misery, purely for His pleasure, that being what we were for, as it were? But if the answer is that He could, and would be right to do so, right being whatever He willed, then one may wonder in what sense He could be said to be loving. Here one may be inclined to say that He can not act like this, justifying this assertion by showing that the actions envisaged would entail some logical inconsistency on God's part. Alternatively, one may allow that a loving God could create a world of misery for His pleasure, for He is loving in some sense which is quite different from that mentioned above. Now it may be the case that misery which is never, even in the long term, beneficial to a person just is that condition which is produced when the person who is experiencing it is somehow in conflict with God's will, so that it would be nonsense to suppose that our purpose as ordained by God was to endure non beneficial misery for His pleasure: any traditional Christian could accept that suggestion, given his general view of the relationship between Creator and creation, and man's place in the scheme of things. But if it is a truth that this is what misery is, it is not a logical truth, for it is logically possible that misery should be accounted for differently. Nor does there seem to be any logical reason why God should not create us in order to destroy us. For one need not hold that to create something necessarily entails that one care for what one has created, though it does seem that one must, in some sense, want it to exist (at least, in circumstances where one is acting rationally, deliberately and freely, bringing something into existence presumably entails wanting it to come into existence). But one need not have a concern for its continued well being. Rather, its well being is a notion which makes sense only in terms of the ends which one has in mind for it. It is not necessarily irrational for people to make things with a view to destroying them, though there are circumstances in which this might be so. But this sort of irrationality occurs when the manner in which one uses what one has made conflicts with the purpose for which one has made it. For example, if one painstakingly translates the *Odyssey* and then proceeds to throw the resulting manuscript on the fire, one would normally be considered to be irrational, since the aim of the exercise was not to produce fuel but something else. But if one spends months building a magnificent edifice out of dominoes and then knocks the entire thing down, one may be quite rational, since the intention all along was to watch its progressive collapse, as each domino displaces the one next to it. (In this context, rationality is teleological: Keneally's portrait of Schindler, the German labour camp commandant who invested a fortune in an entirely unproductive factory in Moravia, maintaining it and its staff and its plant while manufacturing nothing, is not a picture of an irrational man; quite the reverse, for Schindler's purpose was to protect the Jews whom he employed and to confound and deceive the authorities.[20]) It therefore seems likely that it will prove difficult if not impossible to show how there could be any logical reason why God should not create us in order to destroy us, or in order to use us in any way He pleases. With the important proviso that no illogicality be attributed to God, it seems that He could command and thereby make right any action whatever.

Although the divine command theorist might wish to change some of the terms used (arguing that God's commands would always merit the descriptions 'good', 'just', etc.), he will agree with the spirit of Cudworth's conclusion that, from arguments like those of Ockham or Scotus,

> it follows unavoidably, that nothing can be imagined so grossly wicked, or so foully unjust or dishonest, but if it were supposed to be commanded by this omnipotent deity, must needs upon that hypothesis forthwith become holy, just and righteous.

Still, it can be insisted that when it is used to describe God, the term 'loving' does, and must, mean something other than it means in its human applications. If God is omnipotent, omniscient, immutable, timelessly eternal, and impassible, then His love can not be characterized by the sort of feeling for the beloved that characterizes human love. We worry about the ones we love; we hope no harm will befall them; we are moved by their presence and may be grieved by their absence, and so on. Presumably God does not worry or hope or grieve, nor is He moved. It is a commonplace claim in the literature of the philosophy of religion that the language which is used to describe God's relations with His creatures is used analogically rather than literally.[21] But one may argue that there must be some correspondence between divine and human love, else it would be inappropriate to refer to divine love at all. If 'love' meant something wholly different where God's love is concerned then it would make no sense to call it love.[22] Perhaps it will be sufficient to say that what characterizes both divine and human love is a concern for its object. However, that God is concerned about His creatures' condition tells us nothing whatever about what that condition is to be, or what is desired for them, or what their destiny might be. Aquinas says that 'God loves all things, willing them every good they possess', but adds that 'God's love causes the goodness in things, and one thing would not be better than another unless God loved it more'.[23] If the love for a creature is a concern for its good, and if what constitutes its good is whatever God decides shall constitute it, then to describe God as loving amounts to no more than to say that He is concerned with whatever He is concerned with.

Yet the fact that the divine command theorist must allow that God could in principle arrange the world in such a way that what he takes to be his good will prove to be unrealizable, and that God could intend nothing for him other than his ultimate destruction, does not weaken his position. After all, he starts from the premise that unaided reason is insufficient for a full grasp of morality, so he will not consider it to be a problem that unaided reason affords him no logically compelling proof that God can not overthrow the current moral order, or that He will not turn out to be 'loving' in some way wholly at odds with what had been expected. Since his moral theory rests squarely on faith, and he is not chiefly concerned with demonstrating that reason shows that divine command theory *must* be true, but rather with showing that it is (contrary to what his opponents say) consistent with reason and that it therefore *could* be true, he need have no qualms about admitting that what God might do is not necessarily what he believes that He does or will in fact do.

The philosophical challenge to the divine command theorist is to show how his moral theory is consistent, and this much he can do. Just as it is not necessary, in order to demonstrate this, to offer a proof of the existence of God, so it is not necessary to prove that God must deal with His creatures in the manner that men call loving. As it can be taken on faith (in conjunction with the facts of human experience), he may say, that God exists, so it can similarly be taken on faith (combined with experience of the manner in which God has thus far dealt with His creatures) that God is concerned with the good of human beings, where that good is what it is generally taken to be, rather than some illusory or unattainable end. What God's concerns *might* be is not a question that need be considered.

But perhaps the nature of religious belief requires that the faithful should have an absolutely certain basis for holding that God will continue to act in the manner they call good and loving. Morris raises this question.[24] He envisages God as being morally good 'understood basically on the model of human moral goodness' and as essentially bound by moral obligations to act in a particular sort of way. He acknowledges that man may have duties which God does not have (man might have a duty to worship God, but God would have no such duty), and continues:

> Conversely, in virtue of his exalted role *vis-à-vis* the entire universe, God may well have duties shared by no one else, and even duties of which we have no conception. So divine and human duties presumably diverge. But it is a widespread and fundamental religious belief that they must also overlap. If God deigns to communicate with us, he will speak the truth, in accordance with a universal duty. Likewise, if he makes a promise, he will keep it, consistent with another general duty. This area of overlap between human and divine obligation is vital to religious faith. In our ability to know moral principles which bind human conduct we have the ability to anticipate features of divine activity. The belief that such duties as truth telling and promise keeping govern divine conduct grounds the trust the religious believer has in God.

If the goodness of God is accounted for on some human model which admits moral duties then it implies the existence of duties which are binding upon God, which would support the Christian Platonist's case, in its first form outlined above. By *modus tollens*, therefore, and on the account of divine command morality, the absence of any duty that binds God implies that God is not morally good in the sense envisaged by Morris. But this does not weaken the basis of the believer's trust in God. Such trust does not need to be grounded in a belief in divine duties, nor even in a belief that God *must* (must, that is, by nature even if not duty bound) always tell the truth and keep promises, and so on; all that is required is a belief that He *will* keep His promises and tell the truth. The trust in God's future behaviour of those who adhere to the faith can be based on precisely that - faith. And a requirement that something more certain should form the basis of trust could be met by insisting, as some Christians (though not, of course, those who defend divine voluntarism) do, that insofar as His goodness is concerned God necessarily acts - must always act - in the way He has acted and does act: duties do not enter into the matter.

In any case, trust in a person, which is what the Christian's trust in God must be, would not appear to be the sort of thing that is grounded either in necessity or in duty. One's trust that the laws of logic will continue to hold may be grounded in necessity, while one's trust that the bank will give back one's money on demand may be based on one's awareness of a (legal) duty, but these cases differ significantly from the case of one's trust in the continued fidelity of a loved one. And the existence of a moral obligation to act in a certain manner is not in general a sufficient ground upon which to base one's trust that the subject of the obligation will do his duty: it would be strange indeed, given that there are countless instances of obligations unmet, to trust that an agent X *will do* an action Y on the sole ground that X *ought to do* Y. On the contrary, personal trust is more appropriately grounded in the knowledge of a person's character and past actions than in the existence of a duty or a compulsion to act:[25] one feels reasonably sure that one's trusted friend or acquaintance will fulfil some duty not because there is a duty but because one knows that he usually has done his duty or perhaps because he seems virtuous - these amount to the same thing on a duty based model of goodness. But there are people who are untrustworthy, though they still have duties.

In general, the attempt to evade the consequences of divine voluntarism by appealing to aspects of the nature of God, while rejecting anything like independent platonic forms, is a mistaken one. To protest, for any action A, currently taken to be wrong, that God can not do A because He is good is not enough; for His being good consists in His not doing A but in doing other things. Then the protest becomes an assertion that He could not do A because He does not do it, which is plainly a *non sequitur*. And the claim that He somehow has to do good will not stand up in the absence either of binding precepts which would compromise His omnipotence or an adequate account of what it is to be morally necessary. The nature of a creature may be given, but aspects of the nature of the unconstrained and omnipotent Deity are better seen as a function of what He does than as a limiting influence upon His actions. Morris and Menzel argue that necessary truth can be dependent upon God yet not under His control: it stems from His nature.[26] But if aspects of His nature are determined by His actions, rather than the other way about, then there is no absurdity in supposing God to be responsible for them. Omnipotence is conceptually and scripturally central to the traditional account of God in a way that love and goodness, thought of on a human model, are not. Then, with the exception of the doctrine of divine simplicity, there should be no obstacle to conceiving God's nature as in part necessary (that is, His omnipotence) and in part both dependent on His activity and under His control (His goodness and love). A conflict with the doctrine of divine simplicity is far less of a challenge for any account of God's nature than would be a conflict with the doctrine of omnipotence. Even if one accepts Anselm's argument that a composite nature entails some sort of dependence of a being on its parts (as if the being were not identical with those parts) one can hold that this does not apply to different aspects of a nature, that they are not parts of it in any relevant sense.[27] Further, one can argue that it makes no sense to say that aspects of God's nature are the same thing as one another, as would seem to be the case if it is to be conceived of as simple. Omnipotence is logically separate from omniscience; the former may imply the latter but is certainly not implied by it. As Yandell says, it seems 'perfectly possible that something be omniscient but not omnipotent, though this will include knowing how to do things one cannot do';[28] and neither attribute is obviously the same as love or goodness (though love and goodness may in some sense, but not the usual sense, be entailments of omnipotence, as suggested earlier).

A rejection of the doctrine of divine simplicity will also permit the rejection of arguments which rely on it as a means of escaping the *Euthyphro* dilemma, again appealing to God's nature while rejecting independent constraints on God. Kretzmann emphasizes divine simplicity in an attempt to find a middle way between what he calls 'theological objectivism' (the Christian Platonist view according to which there is an independent, objective good to which God's activity conforms) and 'theological subjectivism' (that is, divine voluntarism).[29] On his account, God *is* perfect goodness, and so perfect goodness both sanctions and *is* the criterion of right and wrong. A consideration of the doctrine of divine simplicity is supposed to steer one away from the notion that God has as one of His attributes, and distinct from Himself, the attribute of perfect goodness. Similarly, Stump and Kretzmann write that

> when Aquinas's naturalism is combined with his account of God as absolutely simple, it effects a connection between morality and theology that offers an attractive alternative to divine command morality, construing morality not merely as a dictate of God's will, but as an expression of his nature.[30]

Here, being is identified with goodness, and a thing is good in so far as its potentialities are actualized. God is the supreme being, perfectly actualized, so that His being *is* His goodness. But clearly, if the doctrine of divine simplicity is unsafe then such arguments as these are unsafe too, to the extent that they rely upon it.[31]

But they would fail anyway, even if the doctrine were sound. The attempt to avoid having to refer God's characteristics to some external criterion by locating goodness and perfection in His nature will only succeed if it is already known, without reference to God's activity and will, what goodness and perfection consist in. Yet the concept of perfection and the conception of goodness *as being* (as employed by Stump and Kretzmann, who derive it from Aquinas) are both thoroughly teleological. God is indeed perfect, in the Christian tradition.[32] He lacks nothing and no addition could make Him better. But His lacking nothing and His not being liable to improvement have to be seen in the context of Christian doctrine generally. No doubt He lacks guile, for example; but lacking guile, in a man at any rate, is considered to be a good.[33] It is seen as a perfection, a completeness, equivalent to possessing something that is better, namely honesty. In this context, what counts as a perfection depends upon what is seen, antecedently, as a good. Yandell offers a definition of what he takes as the theist's conception of perfection thus: 'a perfection is the logically maximal degree of a property that has degrees and is better to have than to lack or else an undegreed property it is better to have than to lack'; but, as he adds, *'being a property it is better to have than to lack* cries out for elucidation'.[34]

Artefacts or creatures may be said to be good (or perfect) examples of their kind; and their kind may be instrumental or natural. A perfect artefact will then be one which requires no addition or alteration in order to be used for, or to do, or to be, what it is intended to be used for or what it is intended to do or to be. A creature, similarly, will be good of its kind in so far as it fulfils its natural potential to be what it was created to be: examples of natural kinds are, in a theistic context, dependent upon their creator not only in respect of their actual characteristics but also in respect of the ideal to which they conform when perfect. Their natures, actual or ideal, potential or fulfilled, are ordained by God. And it is difficult to justify any equation of being with goodness unless *being* is taken to mean *being as one (person, thing, state of affairs, etc.) ought to be*.[35] Sheer existence may be a good, in that it is a prerequisite for anything else's being good, but it is again difficult to understand in what sense this could be so, except when such existence is considered instrumentally.[36] And if it is an instrumental good then its goodness is a derivative of the way things ought to be, the way the creation has been ordered by God. In the case of God Himself, if there are no constraints upon Him then it can not be said of Him that He exists in the manner in which He ought to exist, or in the way He is meant to exist, or as He is intended to exist.

Locating God's goodness in His nature as a Trinity of persons fares no better either, for the same sort of reason as that discussed above: unless it is the case both that being a Trinity is a logical necessity for God, and also that being a Trinity logically entails that His nature is good and loving as understood on a human model, then it is again logically possible that He is not a loving Trinity. One could assume for the sake of argument that God must be Trinitarian, or one could take as one's starting point the fact that, in the mainstream tradition of Christianity He just is Trinitarian, and proceed from there in an attempt to show that He is necessarily good and loving as usually understood; but it is not obvious that such an attempt will succeed, and it would in any case amount to a much weaker form of opposition to divine command theory than that of the Christian Platonist. Gunton offers an account which is intended to distance Christian morality from arbitrary divine commands by emphasizing the importance of the Trinity. He suggests that what is required is an Irenaean rather than an Augustinian view of the creation. In Augustine's theology of creation, 'the christological element plays little substantive role, and the pneumatological even less. The result is that the way is laid open for a conception of creation as the outcome of arbitrary will'.[37] On the other hand,

> On an Irenaean account, what holds the creation together... are the Son and the Spirit, by whom the world is held in continuing relation to God the Father. After Augustine that function comes, increasingly, to be performed by the universals, which are traditionally conceived to be a timeless conceptual structure informing otherwise shapeless matter.[38]

He adds that

> Irenaeus' conception of the will of God... sees it as free, but it is not therefore arbitrary and rootless. As important as the concept of will for Irenaeus is that of love... The will of God is realized through a kind of community of love, so that the centrality of the trinitarian mediators of creation ensure the purposiveness of the creation, its non arbitrary character.[39]

However, it is not at all clear why the relationship between the persons of the Trinity should be loving, however such love could be accounted for: rather it might, for example, be something like a relationship of mutual contemplation. Nor is it clear that one can extrapolate from the supposed nature of that relationship to the nature of the creation and its relation to God. The relations within the Trinity are sometimes compared to those within a human family. But such an analogy (and it is a very inexact one) suggests that it is entirely possible that the relationships both between the persons and between them and what they produce can vary. Parents who love each other may detest their offspring, or they may love their offspring while detesting each other. Nor need anything like love be involved in their equivalent to the act of creation, that is, their act of procreation.

There are further difficulties with such an account, not the least of which is that, as Gunton himself remarks, 'trinitarian theology only has point if God is indeed triune, and there is still much to be debated there'.[40] There are, too, Unitarian Christians (such as the pacifist Jehovah's Witnesses) who would wish to stress God's love rather than His power or will.

It is also worth noting that the doctrine of the Trinity is essentially mysterious. Traditional Christian doctrine as maintained by Catholics is referred to in the *Catechism* thus: 'The mystery of the Most Holy Trinity is the central mystery of Christian faith and life. It is the mystery of God in himself. It is therefore the source of all the other mysteries of faith'.[41] The *Catechism* adds:

> In order to articulate the dogma of the Trinity, the Church had to develop her own terminology with the help of certain notions of philosophical origin: 'substance', 'person' or 'hypostasis', 'relation' and so on. In doing this, she did not submit the faith to human wisdom, but gave a new and unprecedented meaning to these terms, which from then on would be used to signify an ineffable mystery, infinitely beyond all that we can humanly understand.[42]

While it may be of religious value, then, the philosophical value of an appeal to a mystery in order to solve a difficulty must be non existent.

Conclusion

It makes no difference to the case of the divine command theorist whether supposedly necessary truths are thought of as entertained by the divine mind or as forming part of the divine nature; whether, in Wolfson's words, the Platonic ideas are 'extradeical' or 'intradeical';[43] whether the Logos is a creation of God or *is* God.[44] Either way, the difficulties of his opponents in explaining *moral* necessity and of reconciling such necessity with divine omnipotence and freedom remain. And when it is granted that creatures' *being*, and not only their *doing*, has a teleological element to it, and that it is God who ordains all the relevant ends, once again those features of divine command theory which at first seemed unacceptable will appear less objectionable, or unobjectionable. Moral action, and its opposite, which in Christian terms is sin, may well appear to be firmly grounded in man's treatment of his fellows, in such a way that God is marginalized or entirely omitted from the account. From the standpoint of liberation theology, Moser and Leers write that one of the main tasks of morality is 'to enable persons and society to be fully themselves';[45] and for Dussel, sin is primarily domination of one's neighbour: 'Offense to God is always and antecedently an act of domination committed against one's brother or sister'.[46] What such claims ignore is what I have argued above, that being fully oneself, and dominating another (in the adverse sense intended by Dussel) take their meaning, in a Christian context, only from a prior understanding of what God intends that people should be. In the terms of divine command theory, therefore, moral action and sin must be seen primarily as obedience and disobedience, respectively, to God.

Notes

1 Cudworth (1731), *Treatise Concerning Eternal and Immutable Morality*, London. The relevant sections, which include all the quotations from Cudworth in this chapter, are reproduced in Idziak (1979), *Divine Command Morality: Historical and Contemporary Readings*, New York, pp. 155-71. There is also a facsimile reprint of the *Treatise* (1976): Garland: New York.

2 One might argue that in such changed circumstances the forbidden action would not in fact be the same as the permitted one. Perhaps it would not; but it would still be the same in all respects relevant to the assertions of the opponents of divine command theory.

3 Alternatively, it could possibly be the case that everything is created in its entire time span, with unchanging properties that imply temporal differences. But in that case, what we think of as change would be illusory; and one of the temporal differences could still be a difference in moral status.

4 What might be termed 'continual re-creation' was a doctrine held by Jonathan Edwards: 'God's upholding created substance, or causing its existence in each successive moment, is altogether equivalent to an immediate production out of nothing, at each moment, because its existence at this moment is not merely in part from God, but wholly from him: and not in any part, or degree, from its antecedent existence' - *Works* Holbrook (1970), Yale, vol. 3, p. 402. This position is criticized by Quinn (1983), 'Divine Conservation, Continuous Creation, and Human Action', in Freddoso, *The Existence and Nature of God*, University of Notre Dame Press. Apart from its moral implications, it implies a view of time as composed of discrete units; this view is what prompts Aristotle to criticize Zeno: 'time is not composed of indivisible instants' (see *Physics*, 239b5 - 240a18). Jonathan Kvanvig and Hugh McCann state what I take to be a traditionally acceptable description of continuous creation: 'As we view the matter, continuous creation should *not* be taken to imply a view that was held by Jonathan Edwards: that each of the things God creates somehow begins to exist *anew* at each moment of its duration... Rather, what is intended is a view according to which each instant of the existence of any of God's creatures is as radically contingent as any other, and equally in need of activity on His part to account for it'. See their (1988) 'Divine Conservation and the Persistence of the World', in Morris, *Divine and Human Action*, Cornell University Press, p. 15.

5   I assume here what I take to be a common sense, though not on that account philosophically unsophisticated view of personal identity. There are of course other views, according to which anyone in another possible world who differs in the slightest respect from me (as I actually am in this world) is not me; but I see no reason to take that view. I discuss the use of the concept of possible worlds at greater length below.
6   Aristotle, *Nicomachean Ethics*, 2, vi.
7   Two actions, X and Y, could be identical except in respect of their moral status, under certain circumstances. If on one occasion X fitted in with God's plan for that period of time then it would be right; yet God's plan for a later period could render action Y wrong. But X and Y might be indistinguishable to anyone but God.
8   Aquinas, *Summa Theologiae*, Ia, 6.3.
9   Plato, *The Laws*, 10, 889.
10 Muirhead (1931), *The Platonic Tradition*, London, chapter three.
11 Such a circumstance may be hard to envisage, but it is a possibility. This is discussed later.
12 On God's immutability see Augustine, *City of God*, XXII, 2, and *De Trinitate*, V, 2, iii; Anselm, *Monologion*, 25; Aquinas, *Summa Theologiae*, Ia, 9.
13 Swinburne (1974), 'Duty and the Will of God', *Canadian Journal of Philosophy* 4, pp. 213-27.
14 This point is discussed further in the section of the next chapter which deals with alternative moral laws.
15 In addition to the account of Abraham and Isaac in Genesis 22 (which is perhaps not a straightforward case, given that God did not allow the killing to proceed) see for example Exodus 12:29.
16 Kierkegaard (1985), *Fear and Trembling*, Penguin Books: London, p. 85.
17 The problems of such a treatment were discussed earlier.
18 Cf. Isaiah 55:8-9; Romans 11:33.
19 See Hick (1990), 'Soul-Making and Suffering', in Adams, M.M. and R.M., *The Problem of Evil*, Oxford: 'The picture [of soul-making] with which we are working is thus developmental and teleological. Man is in the process of becoming the perfected being whom God is seeking to create' - p. 169.
20 Keneally (1982), *Schindler's Ark*, London.
21 This issue is discussed fairly thoroughly in Donovan (1976), *Religious Language*, Sheldon Press: London.
22 For a view which opposes the commonplace position see Clouser (1983), 'Religious Language: A New Look at an Old Problem', in Van der Hoeven and Wolterstorff, *Rationality in the Calvinian Tradition*, University Press of America, pp. 385-407.

23   Aquinas, *Summa Theologiae*, Ia, 20.2,3.
24   Morris (1987), 'Duty and Divine Goodness', in his *The Concept of God*, Oxford, chapter 6. Morris's main concern is to show how God can be both morally good and necessarily good; that is, with how He can have the significant freedom necessary for moral action if He necessarily fulfils (what are assumed to be) His obligations. Such a problem would not arise on my account.
25   'The biblical idea of faith is trust in God *because of what God has done and said* ' - Brown (1968), *Philosophy and the Christian Faith*, London, p. 284; emphasis mine.
26   Morris and Menzel (1986), 'Absolute Creation', *American Philosophical Quarterly* 23, pp. 353-62.
27   Anselm, *Monologion*, 21; *Proslogion*, 20.
28   Yandell, 'Divine Necessity and Divine Goodness', in Morris (1988), op. cit., p. 317.
29   Kretzmann (1983), 'Abraham, Isaac and Euthyphro: God and the Basis of Morality', in Stump, *Hamartia: The Concept of Error in the Western Tradition*, New York.
30   Stump and Kretzmann, 'Being and Goodness', in Morris (1988), op. cit., pp. 281-2.
31   Cf. Morris and Menzel, op. cit., p. 359: 'we believe the doctrine to have serious difficulties which render it unconvincing'. See too Morris (1985), 'On God and Mann: A View of Divine Simplicity', *Religious Studies* 21, pp. 299-318.
32   There are many references in scripture to God's perfections. For some instances see Deut. 32:4; Ps. 18:30 and 19:7; Job 36:4 and 37:16; Mt. 5:48; Rom. 12:2; 2 Sam. 22:31.
33   Cf. Ps. 32:2; John 1:47; 1 Peter 2:22.
34   Yandell, op. cit., ibid. His argument is particularly concerned with existence as a perfection, but what he says applies equally to other perfections.
35   There have been other attempts to effect a connection between being and goodness, in different ways. John Leslie makes such an attempt (1979), *Value and Existence*, Oxford; (1978), 'Efforts to Explain All Existence', *Mind* 87, pp. 181-94; (1980) 'The World's Necessary Existence', *International Journal for the Philosophy of Religion* 11, pp. 207-24. Beyond this footnote I shall not discuss his account, both because what he tries to show would, if true, be completely incompatible with the existence of the personal God of traditional Christianity in His traditional independent state, and also because I agree with J.L. Mackie, who writes that the great difficulty for Leslie's theory 'lies in the implausibility of its own central principle, the hypothesis that objective ethical requiredness

is creative, that something's being valuable can in itself tend to bring that thing into existence or maintain it in existence, and can therefore provide an ultimate explanation for its being there, independently of its being caused or created by any other existing things... it remains a sheer speculation' - (1982), *The Miracle of Theism*, Oxford, p. 237.

36 On the matter of personal existence, Miguel de Unamuno writes thus: 'as a child, I remained unmoved when shown the most moving pictures of hell, for even then nothing appeared to me quite so horrible as nothingness itself' - (1921), *The Tragic Sense of Life in Men and in Peoples*, London, p. 9. Unamuno's attitude may be understandable; but it is of course wholly irrational to hold that a life which contains on balance more bad than good is nevertheless desirable: if any life at all is preferable to none, then this is because something about it is seen as a good to outweigh the bad. Living, too, consists in far more than sheer existence: it seems reasonable to hold that if sheer existence is a good then this is because it is a necessary condition for anything that is good in itself. Further, strictly speaking, nothingness can not *be* horrible; it can not *be* anything at all. Cf. also Aristotle, *Eudemian Ethics* I, 1215b: 'For many of life's events are such that they cause men to throw life away, for instance, diseases, excessive pains, storms; so that it is clear that on account of these things any way it would actually be preferable, if someone offered us the choice, not to be born at all'.

37 Gunton (1993), *The One, The Three and The Many*, Cambridge, p. 54.
38 Op. cit., p. 55.
39 Op. cit., p. 120.
40 Op. cit., p. 7.
41 *Catechism of the Catholic Church* (1994), Vatican, 234, p. 56.
42 *Catechism*, 251, pp. 59-60.
43 Wolfson (1961), *Religious Philosophy*, Cambridge, Mass., chapter 2.
44 For a detailed account of the arguments over this issue in the early church see Wolfson (1970), *The Philosophy of the Church Fathers*, Cambridge, Mass., particularly chapters VII to XV. His account can also be taken to support the claims of those Unitarians who argue that the doctrine of the Trinity has little or no scriptural support but is a later philosophical addition to Christianity as originally practised. This is the claim of Jehovah's Witnesses - see (1990) *Mankind's Search for God*, Watchtower Bible and Tract Society, New York, chapter 11.
45 Moser and Leers (1990), *Moral Theology*, Burns and Oates, p. 56.
46 Dussel (1988), *Ethics and Community*, Burns and Oates, p. 19.

6 Arbitrary commands

Introduction

Here I consider objections to divine command theory which are centred on the claim that it makes the basis of morality arbitrary. This, it is supposed, entails that morality is irrational or liable to be constituted in unacceptable ways. My argument is intended to show that, while arbitrariness is indeed a consequence of the theory, it is nevertheless acceptable.

Arbitrariness

It is sometimes considered to be a major objection to divine command theory that, if it were correct, God's commands would be arbitrary. Brody refers to this argument, observing that there is a commonly held position according to which, if what God commands is good just in virtue of His having commanded it, and it is not the case that He commands a thing because it is good, then 'we would have moral truths based upon the arbitrary desires of God as to what we should do... and this is objectionable'.[1] Meynell, commenting on an argument of Nowell-Smith's, writes that his point is that 'the divine commands must either conform to what is found to be good on other grounds than that God has commanded it, or they must be wholly arbitrary'. Meynell's own position, which suggests a response to this objection which will be taken up later, is quite different, as he makes plain: 'As Nowell-Smith sees it, if God is to be God, his will and commandment must in the last analysis be wholly arbitrary. I would have thought, on the contrary, that if God is to be God, his will and commandment must be supremely reasonable'.[2]

Presumably something more is meant by the claim that God's commands are arbitrary than that they are grounded in His will alone, for this is, precisely, what divine voluntarism consists in - His commands result from the exercise of His *arbitrium*. But before considering what is felt to be amiss with the arbitrariness of divine commands it should be noticed that their arbitrary nature is not a straightforward consequence of their having been issued for some other reason than that what is commanded is good. Bearing in mind that the goodness in question here is moral goodness, it is clear enough that a command need not be related to what is good in order to escape being designated as arbitrary. If I issue the command 'Close the door!', then all that I intend may be to avoid a draught. Still, such commands as this, and perhaps all commands that are not wholly irrational, are in some sense related to the good, in so far as they are intended to bring about some course of action, and that action (or its consequences) is seen as good: if Socrates was right then everything that one pursues is pursued for the sake of some good. Suppose that God commands some action simply because that action will please Him. Then He will have a reason, though not a moral reason, for His command.

There are, however, two difficulties with this account. First, it would be necessary for the divine command theorist to explain how obedience to commands, which had as their basis or object some non moral good, would itself constitute morally good action. Second, such an account, offered in terms of a thing's being pleasing to God, may not deflect the original criticism that morality would somehow be arbitrary: if morality is merely based upon what God happens to like then one may wonder why, on what grounds, He likes it. In our own case, we need not always defend a liking or preference with reasons: a preference for tea rather than coffee, say, may be a result of the way one is constituted, and is not necessarily either to be criticized as irrational or to be explained by reference to rational choice, for it seems not to be the sort of thing to which reasoning need apply. But the matter must be different in the case of an omnipotent being, for if we creatures indeed have no reason for a preference, and it is nothing more than a given fact about the way in which we are constituted, then it is not something over which we have exercised our control; but there is nothing, according to the divine voluntarist account, over which God has not exercised His control (either by directing it, or in the case of creatures' free will, by creating it as it is).

Consider now just what is the objection implicit in the assertion that God's commands are arbitrary if not directed to what is good. When something is described as arbitrary this may be because it is not governed by rules, or is despotic, or capricious. Yet none of these senses of arbitrariness accurately reflects what is felt to be wrong with a morality that is grounded in divine commands. Being governed by rules amounts, usually, to constraint;[3] and it will not be possible for God to be constrained if He is omnipotent. It is in order to avoid this idea of God's being constrained that the divine command theorist insists, in the first place, that He does not command things because they are good, but that, on the contrary, things are good in virtue of His having commanded them. So the objector will not have in mind this sense of arbitrariness if his objection is to amount to anything more than an expression of dissatisfaction with the notion that an almighty being should be free from constraint: what would be required is an account of *why* being free from constraint is objectionable.

Again, when one means that an action is arbitrary in the sense of being despotic, the criticism intended has presumably to do with the fact that the despot's actions are carried out without reference to rules: being despotic does not preclude acting in a caring or enlightened manner - what is generally assumed to be wrong with despotism is that there are no constraints on behaviour, where there ought to be constraints. But the point concerning rule governed behaviour applies here too, so that it can not be a weighty criticism of divine commands that they are despotic if this means no more than that they are made in a manner that is free from constraints.

If the objector to divine command theory is to say that God's behaviour is capricious, then he may mean either that it is whimsical, in the sense that He does whatever He happens to like doing at any particular moment, or he may mean primarily that it is changeable.[4] If the former sense is intended, then bearing in mind the point made above, that what God happens to like can not be a matter that is beyond His control, what is to be explained to the objector is *why* God likes what He likes, or why our inability to answer this question should not be problematic. If it is the changeability of God's commands, or the possibility of such changeability, that the objector wishes to stress then one may suppose that what is objectionable is the lack of good reason for Him to change His commands, for changeability is in itself unobjectionable unless one takes the view, discussed and rejected previously, that God is bound by unchangeable moral rules. (One may be, quite simply, unable to envisage a situation in which moral precepts are other than they now are, and therefore unprepared to accept that God could change them - particularly if one already accepts Christian moral principles and a non voluntaristic version of Christian theology. This problem is discussed below).

Meynell's remark, quoted above, is relevant here: arbitrariness is contrasted with rationality. Similarly, Gunton writes that arbitrariness suggests irrationality.[5] What appears to underlie the objection to divine command theory, when it is said that God's commands are arbitrary if the theory is correct, is the unacceptability of the notion that God's behaviour is, or could be, irrational, if not actually in itself then to our way of thinking. It is difficult, if not impossible, to understand why He commands what He does command. At this point one could give up the attempt to offer further explanation, arguing that of necessity there will be things that creatures can not understand about their Creator, but perhaps this limit of explanation has not yet been reached. Before considering what reason there could be for God's commands to be as they are if divine command theory is true, it is worth examining what sort of rationality He is to be credited with.

It can safely be asserted that God can not do what is illogical: this has been shown earlier, when it was argued that the inability to bring about a logical contradiction was no restriction of God's omnipotence. Consider next the rationality of means and ends. One is irrational if one uses in the attempt to achieve an end any means which one knows will not in fact achieve it. But God can not will as a means to an end something which He knows will not work; for willing as a means entails willing that the means in question will achieve the desired end, and if God is omnipotent then what He wills as a means *is* a means to whatever end He has, providing that it is logically possible that the means can bring about the end. God can not then have as a desired end human happiness, say, while at the same time willing that, as a means to this end, humans should behave in a way that rules out the possibility of the achievement of happiness. If He wills happiness for us then He can not command an action that precludes it: given (as has been argued earlier) that He intends His commands to be obeyed, and that He wills that the state of affairs entailed by such obedience should obtain, this would be tantamount to willing contradictory ends.

Now consider the rationality of ends. An end is irrational if its realization would be logically impossible; or if its realization prevents the realization of another end that is more highly valued; or, simply, if there is no reason for it. It is clear that God's ends can not be irrational in the first of these ways. For, although a man could, in a sense, set his sights on achieving what was a logical contradiction, this possibility exists only because men's knowledge is limited: only through ignorance of the fact that there is no such thing as a square circle could a man put himself in the frame of mind of trying to construct one. But God is omniscient, so it makes no sense to suppose that He can aim to realize something that is, logically, unrealizable - there would be literally nothing, *no thing*, at which He would aiming, since there can be no square circles or any other logically contradictory constructions. Nor can His ends be irrational in the second way. For if God is omnipotent, then if He has two ends, He can realize both of them. The realization of one of His ends can prevent the realization of the other only if the two ends are logically incompatible. But to will two such ends would be to will an inconsistency, and this has already been ruled out as impossible for God to do.

More analysis is required in the third case. All reasoning stops somewhere: in our own case we may give as a reason for engaging in a certain activity the fact that it makes us happy. If pressed for a reason why we should want to be happy then we should perhaps be inclined to regard the question as misplaced. We may say that no further reason is needed, and that happiness just is what we want; and we may wonder what sort of reason there could ever be over and above this. Yet the pursuit of happiness will not be condemned as irrational. Then it seems that the stopping point in our chain of reasoning can be reached when we say that we want something, that it makes us happy. When, as sometimes happens, it is claimed that a person did something 'for no reason at all', what is often meant is that the person had no reason other than wanting to do the deed. We do not, it appears, do things for no reason *at all* unless our action is not deliberate, and is therefore beyond the control of our will. If, for example, we condemn as being without reason a sudden act of violence which seems quite pointless to us, then - unless we mean only that it has no reason which we consider acceptable - we are apt to be mistaken: assuming that there is no hidden reason of which we are unaware, then the culprit was violent either for no other reason than that he wanted to be violent, or else his behaviour was not subject to his will, and not morally blameworthy. This line of argument suggests that the third form of irrationality of ends does not have any instances in the case of willed behaviour.

Now, if doing something because we want to is not in itself irrational, if, that is, wanting something provides an acceptable stopping point in our chain of reasoning, then some similar state of affairs can reasonably be held to obtain where God is concerned: that God wills to act in a certain way will be a sufficient reason for Him to act in that way. Since, too, none of God's acts is outside the control of His will (for to be so would be at odds with His omnipotence), the conclusion that can now be reached is this. God can not be irrational in any of the ways considered here. It follows that God's commands can not be arbitrary in any of the senses intended to convey criticism, though they are, of course, arbitrary in the literal sense implied by divine voluntarism. 'Our God is in the heavens; he does whatever he pleases', says Aquinas;[6] and the divine command moralist's insistence that this entails that God commands whatever He pleases implies no irrationality on His part.

Alternative divine commands

If divine command theory entails the possibility that God's commands could have been wholly different from those commands which traditional Christianity accepts, then the divine command theorist must be prepared to show how this could be so without producing what might appear to be a complete subversion of morality itself, and how it could be consistent with essential aspects of Christian moral teaching. The bare possibility that God might have commanded what Christians and, indeed, adherents of other moral theories, believe to be so morally repugnant that it is unimaginable is sometimes raised almost as a *reductio ad absurdum* of what is taken to be the excessiveness of the voluntarist version of divine command morality, the theory as embraced by Duns Scotus, for example; and yet that possibility does not amount to such a *reductio*, as closer examination will show.[7]

There are two aspects to this issue: the divine command theorist can offer arguments which show that there are no morally necessary precepts such as those envisaged by Cudworth and other Christian Platonists - this aspect has already been discussed earlier. But notwithstanding these arguments, there may remain a deep seated opposition to the claims of the voluntarist account caused by an intuition that, while it might be logically possible for God to issue wholly different commands, the result would not be morality in any recognizable sense. The argument below is directed more towards this latter aspect of the issue: if he can show how, plausibly, very different divine commands would still produce what is generally meant by morality, then the divine command moralist will have his case greatly strengthened.

Scotus's position (like that of Ockham discussed earlier) can be taken as a representative example of the most extreme form of divine command theory, in the sense that his account of divine voluntarism acknowledges no restrictions upon God's possible actions other than restrictions of logic. According to Scotus,[8] lying or killing could be legitimate if God revoked the precepts which forbid them, and could be meritorious if He commanded them. He also argues that 'the justice of God will be coextensive with the power of God', so that anything which He can do, which is anything at all not involving a contradiction, will be just; for

> the divine will, which is the first rule of all works and of all acts, and the activity of the divine will, of which the first rule consists, is the first principle of righteousness. For from the fact that something is suitable to the divine will, it is right; and whatever action God could perform, is right absolutely.

Even if God damns someone who is just, He acts justly; and the same is true if He saves someone who is unjust.[9] Mann develops an interpretation of Scotus's views according to which creation has no value in itself:

> God's will does not operate by acknowledging the good making intrinsic properties of things; his will establishes what properties *count* as good making. Analogous remarks apply to badness or evil. God could have created a world whose inhabitants are incapable of scientific discovery, aesthetic appreciation, and moral sentiment, who are exquisitely sensitive to the pain to which they are perpetually subjected, and who rise above that pain solely to inflict torture on helpless animals. Had God declared that world to be good, ipso facto it would have been good. Had he 'seen' that the actual world, the world he did create, was very rotten, it would have been very rotten. Any world God picks can have any dimension of value he declares it to have, just in virtue of his act of declaration. The pursuit of wisdom is a good thing, but it might have been replaced by the practice of sadism. Charity is a virtue, but in some possible worlds hardness of heart is the summum bonum.[10]

The horrified reaction to this extreme form of divine voluntarism is exemplified by Adams:

> Suppose God should command me to make it my chief end in life to inflict suffering on other human beings, for no other reason than that he commanded it... Will it seriously be claimed that in that case it would be wrong for me not to practise cruelty... ?[11]

Ewing's remark indicates a similar response to the same form of divine voluntarism: 'Since there was no ethical reason for his commands, God might in that case just as well command us to cheat, torture and murder, and then it would really be our duty to act like this'.[12]

In attempting to show that the consequences of views such as those of Scotus are neither repugnant nor incompatible with traditional Christianity, the divine command theorist must consider precisely what the traditional teaching consists in; and this is not straightforward, since there are apparent contradictions both in the writings of different Christian moralists and also, sometimes, in different works of the same author. Anselm writes: 'For that alone is just which thou [i.e., God] dost will; and that alone unjust which thou dost not will'.[13] But elsewhere[14] he writes that when it is said that what God wishes is just, and that what He does not wish is unjust, we must not understand that if God wished anything improper it would be just, simply because He wished it; for if God wishes to lie, we must not conclude that it is right to lie, but rather that he is not God, 'for no will can ever wish to lie, unless truth be impaired'. But he adds that if God wishes that a man should die, then it is right that he die.

Suarez argues that God must be able to grant dispensations from the natural law; but he then divides the precepts of natural law into three types, the most universal sort (e.g., that one may not do evil, one must pursue good), immediate consequences of these (e.g., the precepts of the decalogue), and other, more remote precepts, and says that God can not grant dispensations from the first type.[15]

Abelard[16], whose concern is to show that the intention of the moral agent is what determines the moral status of his acts, argues that all actions are in themselves morally indifferent, and that this is shown by the fact that 'works which it is or is not at all fitting to do may be performed as much by good as by bad men who are separated by their intention alone'. He adds,

> In fact, the same thing is often done by different people, justly by one and wickedly by another, as for example if two men hang a convict, that one out of zeal for justice, this one out of a hatred arising from an old enmity... yet, through the diversity of their intention, the same thing is done by diverse men, by one badly, by the other well.

On the other hand, Price writes:

> If all actions and all dispositions of beings are in themselves indifferent, the all perfect understanding of the deity, without doubt, perceives this; and therefore he cannot approve, or disapprove of any of his own actions, or of the actions of his creatures: The end he pursues, and the manner in which he treats his creatures must appear to him what it is - indifferent. What foundation then is left for his moral perfections? How can we perceive him

to pursue universal happiness as his end, when, at the same time, we suppose nothing in the nature of that end to engage the choice of any being? Is it no diminution of his perfect character, to suppose him guided by mere unintelligent inclination, without any direction from reason, or any moral approbation?[17]

and added, in a different edition, is the remark: 'It being a contradiction to approve or disapprove, where it is known that there is nothing in itself right or wrong'[18].

Even from the writings of Aquinas, whose views on moral and theological matters have been considered definitive by many Christians, it is not easy to extract a single, unambiguous doctrine about what God could or could not do by way of making alterations in the moral status of actions. Like Suarez, he distinguishes different levels of moral precepts, and argues that 'the first premises of the law that is in us by nature are altogether unalterable'.[19] Yet he allows for the possibility that God could command us to engage in what we should normally term murder, theft and adultery, by proposing that such actions cease to be murder, theft and adultery when commanded by God.[20] 'Whatever God commands in the world of human affairs is just'; and God's will is in a sense not subject to the eternal law, yet in a different sense subject to it:

> As to God's will, if by that we mean the will itself, identical with God, then it is not subject to the eternal law but is itself the law; but if we mean by God's will what God wills for creation, then that is subject to the law as to God's wise plan.[21]

The diversity within and between Christian moralists or apologists reflects an ambivalence to be found in the very scriptural basis of Christianity: on the one hand, God is the Just One;[22] on the other hand, men have no grounds for complaint against God whatever He should do.[23] Abelard would find little difficulty in finding scriptural support for his claim that

> however God wishes to treat his creature he cannot be accused of injustice. And what happens in accordance with his will can in no sense be called evil. We can only distinguish good from evil according as it is in agreement with his will and consists in his good pleasure. No one can have the presumption to find fault with what appears to be the worst of reprehensible behaviour when it is done at the Lord's command... Our conclusion is... that nothing should be called well done or ill done except it be in accordance with, or contrary to, his excellent will.[24]

Some of the points raised above can be dealt with without considering what the world would be like if God had issued completely different moral precepts;

others will be better addressed after such a state of affairs has been considered. There is some reason to suppose that the nature of Christian belief will give rise to difficulties in determining whether or not the moral status of a given act is unchangeable. For Christians hold that man is imperfect, both in his reasoning about, and in his knowledge of, moral matters; that he is unworthy of whatever God gives him, and has no claim as of right to any particular treatment at God's hands. If we can never be entirely sure of our judgment concerning a moral issue, if there always remains the possibility that God, who is omniscient, has access to information denied to us and powers of reasoning which infinitely surpass our own, and if we are in any case undeserving, then we may be mistaken about the unchangeable moral status of an act: what we think of as justice may, with greater insight, be seen to be something else, and what we expect by way of just treatment from God may not be what we ought to receive. Nevertheless, along with everyone else, Christians have to rely upon their judgment, treating it as if it were wholly dependable, both because acting morally would otherwise prove impractical or impossible and also because for them, at least, moral judgment is in part based upon what is taken to be the revealed word of God. But it must be admitted that there is room for error, in some circumstances, in making moral judgments, and this may go some way towards explaining why there should be, in the Christian tradition, some diversity of opinion about the nature of certain aspects of morality. In seeking to show that his theory is compatible with the Christian tradition, the divine command theorist can therefore bear in mind that the difficulty in identifying precisely what that tradition involves is to be expected: he may prove unable to satisfy everyone.

Part of the diversity within the tradition results not from disagreement over fundamental issues, but from a difference of emphasis or from considering different aspects of moral law. In considering what Aquinas and Suarez take as primary precepts of natural law, the status of moral precepts as unchangeable is foremost. In considering whether and how more remote precepts are derivable from primary precepts, more attention may be given to circumstances which indicate the possibility that precepts are not absolute, and to arguments which suggest that actions are in themselves morally indifferent. As a matter of logic, given what the term 'morality' means and what morality is all about, the primary moral precepts, that good is to be pursued and that evil is to be avoided, are unchangeable: anything else would not be morality. This is quite consistent with the view that acts in themselves have no moral status, for 'pursuing good' and 'avoiding evil' would on that view be terms too general to qualify as descriptions of acts. Similarly, as a matter of logic, if 'good' means, or is ultimately to be accounted for only as, 'in accordance with the will of God', then God can not command creatures to do anything other than good, whatever particular action He commands. Neglecting this point, neglecting for instance that the Thomist's use of the term 'good' might at times refer to man's good *as ordained by God*, will result in the discovery of disagreements where none really exists; and the views of

Scotus and of Price, for example, might be found to be compatible once it has been established precisely what claims are being made. Clearly one important part of the procedure to be adopted in deciding whether or not an action's moral status is changeable is the determination of what constitutes an action in this context; in particular, determining whether or not the naming of an action includes a reference, not necessarily explicit, to the will of God or to the intention of the agent, might be crucial.

It should be noted too that the consequences of divine voluntarism are not what they are sometimes alleged to be. The interpretation of Scotus's position which is offered by Mann is not a correct characterization of what divine voluntarism entails, so that the problem it seems to pose for the divine command theorist is not one that he need in fact consider. It is one thing to assert that, subject to the restrictions of logic, God can command or forbid any action whatever, and that actions are in this way made morally good or bad; it is quite another matter to assert that 'any world God picks can have any dimension of value he declares it to have, just in virtue of his act of declaration'. If this latter state of affairs were a consequence of divine voluntarism then voluntarism would indeed be difficult to defend, for it would entail that moral value had no meaning: God's labelling of world X as valuable and world Y as worthless would amount to no more than an act of naming, in which the names denoted nothing at all - in fact, both worlds could be identical apart from their names. The opponent of divine command theory could then argue that to act as if such value naming had any implications for behaviour would be irrational, either for God or for a creaturely moral agent. It simply makes no sense to suppose that value can be assigned in this way, in the absence of any possible explanation of what it is to be valuable, other than to say that it is no more than to be called 'valuable'. What the divine voluntarist holds is that moral value attaches to actions which are prescribed by God for a moral agent: it is action in accordance with God's will that is valuable, whatever that action should happen to be. Thus he would not hold that God could create a world without moral agents in it and then deem it worthless: if God is rational then He creates because He in some way wants that creation brought about. And in the absence of significantly free moral creatures, everything that happens in His created world is a direct result of His action, or rather, it *is* His action, and it must be in accordance with His will. A man can 'create', as it is sometimes put, a work of art - a painting, for instance, and be dissatisfied with the result; but he can not sensibly be said simply to label it as unsatisfactory and by that act lessen its value. Further, that it is unsatisfactory is due to some lack of ability on his part, a failure to do what he intended or a failure to match an ideal; and in this respect he lacks some ability even if the deficiencies in the painting are caused by some defect in the materials used rather than in his own talent for painting. God can not fail in this way: what He creates He must, if He is unconstrained and rational, somehow 'see' as good, that is, as what He wants. If He 'sees' anything as bad then presumably the cause of its badness must lie in a free moral agent who acts in a way that God does not directly will, though He permits it. The actions commanded or forbidden by God could be, for all we know, arbitrary; but that is not to say that God arbitrarily assigns value by the act of declaring something to be valuable. For the divine command theorist, as noted above, a morally valuable action is one done in accordance with God's will; but God's motive in choosing which actions to command and which actions to forbid is not strictly relevant here. It might be that what God wants of us is no more than freely given obedience, and that could be the stopping point in a chain of reasoning, the point at which no further explanation can be given. But it is false to claim, as Price does, that without a moral motive God has no reason to act, for He may have either a non moral motive or one which it is beyond our ability to grasp. One could perhaps argue that it is in the nature of an omnipotent being (which God must be if He is to be God) to require obedience and, what follows, to permit freedom; but any explanation of this sort goes beyond what is necessary for a defence of divine voluntarism.

Consider now the type of action that is sometimes alleged to have unchangeable moral status, and also what would follow from the alteration of certain moral precepts. Torturing children for fun is an action held by, among others, Swinburne[25] to be unchangeably wrong: no possible circumstance, no divine decree, could make it morally right, ever. It is an action which involves a number of factors, including the infliction of pain, an innocent victim, an unwilling victim, no good end or intention, and, given that it involves children rather than some other human or animal, perhaps the strongest offence against normal instinct. This last point is worth making if only to draw attention to the possibility that the revulsion felt by a normal person at the thought of such torture, or at the idea that it could possibly be morally right, may be, in part at least, so deeply connected with instinct and emotion that one would continue in the attempt to justify one's attitude to it even if one's position had been shown to be irrational. However that may be, it is not self evidently true that torture is wrong in all circumstances. It could certainly be justified with a degree of plausibility on utilitarian grounds, if it were undertaken for the common good and likely to be effective in achieving it. If information necessary for the very survival of one's immediate society, or society as a whole, could only be obtained by torturing one's enemy then there would be a utilitarian case to be made in favour of torture; nor need it be of much relevance to the calculation that the victim was innocent. The factor most obviously relevant in the case of torturing children for fun is presumably the absence of a good end or intention; that is, either the torturer has a bad intention, or the entire action is undertaken for no good reason. If a surgeon has to inflict pain on a child by, say, carrying out an operation to save the child's life, when no anaesthetic is available, then he does the right thing, no doubt, even though the child is innocent and unwilling, and the act offends all the instincts of an observer. Suppose that the surgeon takes pleasure in inflicting pain in these circumstances, and acts with that pleasure as the end he has in view: if we wish now to condemn on moral grounds what occurs then this can only be because 'what occurs' includes the intention of the agent. We condemn him for his bad intention or his wrongful motive. But if that is our only reason for condemning him then it is clear in this case, a case deliberately intended by Swinburne and others to be, on account of its extreme nature, an example of something always and undeniably wrong, that the unchangeable moral status of the action is only to be admitted after due consideration of the end of the action or the intention of the agent. Then the action *in itself* can be thought of as being morally indifferent: what one intends to convey by *action in itself* may be only what is observable, let it be supposed, in which case the surgeon's state of mind forms no part of it.

Now the importance of ends and intentions is precisely what the divine command theorist will wish to stress. While holding that acts in themselves are morally indifferent, he claims that the proper end of an action is a matter which is determined by God, and that the intention to conform to the divine will is by definition a good intention. Thus if God should decree that the purpose of the life of some particular child is to suffer pain, then so be it. In the light of the knowledge of other facts about the way God has created the child and those people who form relationships with him, such a decree might be irrational or illogical, involving some inconsistency or contradiction, some frustration of, or impediment to, His overall plan; but then it would not be possible for God to issue it.

There are concepts which we need to accept if human life is to function, yet which can not be described as necessary in the sense of being logically necessary - they are not concepts the rejection of which entails a contradiction. These might include the concepts of space and time, for example. Yet posited morally necessary precepts do not appear to be in this category: it is at least imaginable that inflicting pain on an innocent should be in accordance with the will of God, and that it can therefore be undertaken wholeheartedly and for pleasure without transgressing any moral law. The aspect of this that is scarcely imaginable, what *seems* irrational, is that we should be commanded or permitted to act in ways which seriously violate our fundamental, instinctive beliefs. Just as it would be unacceptable for us to be required to violate our rational beliefs at God's behest (it would be unacceptable precisely because irrational), so would it be unacceptable if we were to be required to violate other, non rational but essentially human aspects of our personality at His command (because such action would be, strictly, non human). What follows, if God's rational nature is to be preserved, is that we must assume either that God would not command or permit torture for pleasure without first bringing about some fundamental change in our nature;[26] or that if He did command or permit it, while our nature remained as it now is, then He had some good reason which was beyond our power to grasp. We are not entitled to rule out a priori any such divine command or permission, however.

A world in which free agents rightly inflict pain is imaginable;[27] what is not imaginable is that it should be right to inflict it when it is not for the good. Yet what constitutes the good needs to be explained: torture could be defensible, in

Christian terms just as in utilitarian terms, if certain conditions were met. The position imagined by Swinburne to be a disproof of divine voluntarism is problematic only because it is described in terms which disguise the fact that what is being claimed is just this: that it can never be right to inflict pain in circumstances which make it wrong. This is not to say that circumstances can never be altered in such a way that it ceases to be wrong, for what constitutes the good of the person suffering pain is a circumstance which is determined by God.

What the divine command theorist can argue, then, is that God can alter the ends for which His creatures were made so that the status of actions as either morally right or morally wrong is altered too. He can also argue that his account is compatible with the traditional doctrine that certain acts are unalterably or intrinsically wrong, provided that doctrine is understood correctly. Such acts fall into one of two categories:

1. Either they are acts which involve, necessarily, a departure from the divine will (the act of disobeying God, for example) or they are actions which as a matter of logic or meaning are described in such a way that they are always wrong (Murder is wrongful killing, so it is always wrong, but killing is not always wrong). In these cases logic prescribes that the acts involved are always wrong, and this is entirely compatible with the position of the divine voluntarist.

2. Other acts described as intrinsically wrong are admitted by tradition. Aquinas identifies actions whose wrongness is a necessary consequence of their 'material object',[28] by which he means, as Mahoney explains, the act apart from intention and circumstance, the 'moral stuff out of which the action is fashioned', the very material, as it were, of the act itself.[29] Similarly Pope John Paul II asserts the view of a large body of traditionalists when he says of intrinsically evil acts that they are wrong 'always and per se... on account of their very object [i.e., Aquinas's 'material object'], and quite apart from the ulterior intentions of the one acting and the circumstances'.[30] However, this intrinsic wrongness is itself defined in relation to the divinely ordered end for man. What both Aquinas and Pope John Paul II intend is the condemnation, the ruling out as utterly disordered in God's plan, of certain acts, *given* the actual ends God has ordained for men. *Given* human nature as it is, nothing could make right certain actions which always impede or prevent its proper development and flourishing.[31] Again, the divine voluntarist can accept this, for he merely seeks to point out that omnipotent God could have ordained some other end for man.

Nor should it be supposed that the divine command theorist's explanation of the manner in which torture could be made morally acceptable entails any contravention of the traditional precept that one may not do evil that good may come of it.[32] For clearly, in the circumstances envisaged, one would not be committing an evil act in order to realize some future good, but actually doing good, since one's act would itself be good, having been sanctioned by God. In any event, even without a new divine decree permitting it, the mere infliction of pain should not be regarded as an evil. We are not entitled to do evil in order to bring about good, but we are entitled to inflict pain in order to bring about good. The Thomist view of pains (and pleasures, for that matter)[33] is that these are neither good nor bad in themselves, but derive any moral status they may have from circumstances and intentions. To this extent, then, the consequences of the voluntarism espoused by the divine command theorist are entirely compatible with the mainstream tradition of Christian moral thought; and those non Christians or atheists who accept that traditional theism *could* be true will accept that the concept of divinely ordained ends prevents voluntarism's consequences from subverting morality altogether. Whatever God should command, though it might involve hurting His creatures, it could never involve harming them, since harm is to be accounted for in terms of divinely ordained ends: anything which detracts from a creature's ability to achieve those ends is harmful.

Understanding God

Mahoney writes that Christian theology is 'an act of faith in the ultimate intelligibility and self consistency of God, and a stumbling attempt to comprehend something of the mystery which one believes is not at heart an intellectual absurdity or sheer caprice'.[34] Gunton discusses the suggestion that the account of God which stresses His power and will to the exclusion of other of His attributes denies us any insight into the rationality of creation.[35] (Though these two writers share a conviction that divine voluntarism has unpalatable consequences, their approaches differ: they both wish to avoid any account of God's actions which makes them arbitrary, but Mahoney is arguing for a more rational account of the moral law while Gunton is seeking to provide an account of God which emphasizes His Trinitarian nature. Each account is put forward as giving us a better insight into the nature of creation, including within that a better insight into morality and the good).

It has already been shown that much of the criticism directed against the claim that God's commands are arbitrary is misplaced, and that arbitrariness does not imply caprice, or anything irrational. Likewise the suggestion, that the divine command moralist's account denies us any insight into the nature of God or the rationality of the creation, is mistaken. It is not as if there were only two alternatives in the matter: either we creatures understand the reasons why God chooses to arrange moral affairs in the manner He does, and therefore understand why He has the ends He has, or else we have no insight into His reasoning nature or into the way He has ordered His creation. On the contrary, we can accept divine command theory and apply our reason to the commands which God has issued, and thus discern in some measure what He is like, what His nature is in certain respects. We have on the one hand our knowledge of revealed divine decrees, and on the other hand our knowledge of human nature and our experience of the world. We can reason about how these fit together, and also, given these, about what God's purposes for creation are likely to be. An analogy may help to make the point: if I visit someone's house and examine the contents, the interior decoration, the layout of the rooms and so forth, then I can perhaps make fairly accurate inferences about the character of the occupier. I might be able to reason out various pieces of information concerning his tastes in art, music and food, and something of his habits. But I will be unable to make any inference about why he likes what he likes, and not some other thing, or about why his habits are thus rather than so. Similarly with my insight into the nature of God and the creation: the scope for the application of my reason is great, but such reasoning may lead me no nearer to the answer to the question why God has the purposes or ends He does have.

Conclusion

What has been argued above is first, that some of the supposedly objectionable features of human arbitrariness can not be features of God's arbitrariness and second, that a thorough appreciation of the manner in which, in reasoning about human ends, the stopping point in a chain of reasoning is reached enables us to understand how the arbitrary nature of divine commands does not preclude their being rationally acceptable. If an objector to divine command theory continues to be dissatisfied with an account according to which God's pleasure, so to speak, is made the foundation of morality - perhaps arguing that there is nothing particularly moral about all this - then he should be reminded that, whatever morality is based upon, the ultimate criterion of the good must be something that is non moral. As Brown observes, in order to avoid an infinite regress 'it follows that the very possibility of morality depends upon the possibility of having an ethical criterion which was not adopted by passing a moral judgement on it'.[36] In the absence of a divine Creator, it would not appear to be implausible to base morality upon the happiness of human beings - which would amount in fact to no more than basing it upon what people happened to like. Indeed some atheistic accounts of morality are precisely of this kind. Then if the core belief of traditional Christianity is correct, if Almighty God exists, such objectors ought to be prepared to accept an account which accords to His pleasures the place given to man's pleasures in corresponding atheistic accounts. Douglas writes of the interpretations of the dietary laws in Leviticus, chapter eleven, that they 'fall into one of two groups: either the rules are meaningless, arbitrary because their intent is disciplinary and not doctrinal, or they are allegories of virtues and vices'.[37] But on the divine command account of morality *all* commands of God are fundamentally arbitrary (though not therefore meaningless) in that even those, such as certain of the commands of the decalogue, which coincide with what is prescribed by rational self interest or which are conducive to virtue, could have been other than they are and depend only upon the will of God: what counts as self interest, what counts as virtue, are matters that have themselves been freely decided by God, and could have been determined otherwise. But Douglas's reference to the disciplinary purpose of commands is relevant, for if what God requires is no more than obedience to His will, whatever that may be, then the content of His commands is unimportant: all that is important morally is whether we obey or disobey His instructions, and the sole purpose of His instructions could be a disciplinary one, in that they set us a discipline, a set of rules for living by, in order to provide an opportunity for showing obedience.[38]

Notes

1   Brody (1981), 'Morality and Religion Reconsidered', in Helm, *Divine Commands and Morality*, Oxford.
2   Meynell (1972), 'The Euthyphro Dilemma', *Proceedings of the Aristotelian Society*, supplementary volume. The argument he discusses is in Nowell-Smith (1966), 'Morality: Religious and Secular', in Ramsey, *Christian Ethics and Contemporary Philosophy*, London.
3   One can impose rules upon oneself, but in such a circumstance one can hardly be said to be constrained by them (cf. Dworkin's remarks, quoted earlier). The question whether God's nature can possibly constrain His will has been discussed above.
4   Traditionally, God can not change His mind, as it were, since He is held to be immutable. 'Eternity principally characterizes God who is utterly unchangeable' - Aquinas, *Summa Theologiae*, Ia, 10. But that doctrine is consistent with divine commands changing from time to time, since God can eternally will change while not changing His will.
5   Gunton (1993), *The One, The Three and The Many*, Cambridge, p. 122.
6   Aquinas, *Summa Theologiae*, Ia, 19.6. The reference is taken from Psalm 115:3.
7   'A standard objection to this theory - let's call it the arbitrariness objection - has long been that it cannot escape the following dilemma. On the one hand, if God has no reason for what He commands, then His commands - and hence morality as well, according to the theory - are fundamentally arbitrary. On the other hand, if God does have reasons for what He commands, then it is those reasons rather than divine commands on which morality ultimately depends. The first horn of the dilemma *is said to be too implausible to be acceptable*; the second, to abandon the divine-command theory itself.' - Sullivan (1993), 'Arbitrariness, divine commands, and morality', *Philosophy of Religion* 33, pp. 33-45; emphasis mine.
8   Duns Scotus (1891-5), 'Quaestiones in Libros Sententiarum', in *Works*, Paris.

9	For a less voluntaristic interpretation of Scotus's position see Copleston (1953), *A History of Philosophy*, London, vol. 2, pp. 544-51.
10	Mann (1991), 'The Best of All Possible Worlds', in MacDonald, *Being and Goodness*, Cornell University Press.
11	Adams (1987), *The Virtue of Faith*, Oxford, pp. 98-9.
12	Ewing (1961), 'The Autonomy of Ethics', in Ramsey, *Prospect for Metaphysics*, London.
13	Anselm, *Proslogion*, xi.
14	Anselm, *Cur Deus Homo*, i, 12.
15	Suarez (1944), *De Legibus*, London, p. 286.
16	Abelard (1971), *Ethics*, Luscombe (ed.), Oxford, p. 29.
17	Price (1974), *A Review of the Principal Questions in Morals*, Raphael (ed.), Oxford, p. 49.
18	See footnote in Raphael's edition, op. cit., p. 49.
19	Aquinas, *Summa Theologiae*, Ia IIae, 94.5.
20	Aquinas, op. cit., ibid. See too Augustine, *City of God*, I, 21, and *Questions on the Heptateuch*, II, 39.
21	Aquinas, op. cit., Ia IIae, 93.4.
22	Acts 7:52.
23	Romans 9:20-21.
24	Abelard, *Super Epist. ad Rom.*, 2,6.
25	Swinburne (1986), *The Coherence of Theism*, Oxford, pp. 186-7. See too Quinn (1990), 'The Recent Revival of Divine Command Ethics', *Philosophy and Phenomenological Research*, supplement, pp. 345-65.
26	Cf. the position of Ockham. See Copleston (1953), *A History of Philosophy*, London, vol. 3, p. 104: 'God could not create *the particular kind of being which we call man* and impose on him precepts irrespective of their content'; (emphasis mine).
27	There is an interesting example of what the imagination can produce in the way of rightful torture in Orson Scott Card's novel (1991), *Xenocide*, London.
28	Aquinas, op. cit., Ia IIae, 18.6.
29	Mahoney (1987), *The Making of Moral Theology*, Oxford, p. 179.
30	Pope John Paul II (1993), *Veritatis Splendor*, Vatican, p. 98.
31	Cf. Dedek (1983), 'Intrinsically Evil Acts: The Emergence of a Doctrine', *Recherches de Theologie Ancienne et Medievale* 50, pp. 191-226: 'St. Thomas Aquinas knew nothing of intrinsically evil acts, that is, physical acts which are so morally disordered in themselves that they never can be good or licit in any circumstances or for any purpose. Thomas spoke only of acts which are *secundum se* evil and therefore never can be made good or licit even by God... Acts which are *secundum se* evil already are defined in moral terms... But no material action... is so inherently

deformed that it cannot be permitted or commanded by God for a good reason'. See also Dedek (1979), 'Intrinsically Evil Acts: An Historical Study of the Mind of St. Thomas', *The Thomist* 43, pp. 385-413.

32 Romans 3:8.
33 Aquinas, op. cit., Ia IIae, 34.1.
34 Mahoney, op. cit., p. 246.
35 Gunton, op. cit., p. 57.
36 Brown (1968), 'Religious Morality: A Reply to Flew and Campbell', *Mind* 77, pp. 577-80.
37 Douglas (1979), *Purity and Danger*, London, p. 43.
38 There is an element in the Jewish tradition which accords with this view. Sokol mentions a Talmudic interpretation (Berakot 33b) which holds that 'God's reason for legislating the moral laws was not the morality of the law; his purpose was merely to promulgate (what could in fact be arbitrary) decrees, so as to demand obedience from man solely on account of the divine origin of the decree' - Sokol (1986), 'The Autonomy of Reason, Revealed Morality and Jewish Law', *Religious Studies* 22, pp. 423-37.

7 Conclusion

It might still be thought that the defence of a Scotist or Ockhamist account of morality is a defence of a position so extreme as to remain deeply implausible. Doubt about the tenability of the account I have offered may be prompted by differing considerations. An atheist might suppose that a defence of divine command theory amounts to an unacceptable moral argument for the existence of God; a moral rationalist might conclude that such a defence mistakenly eliminates or restricts the proper role of reason in determining moral duties, and contradicts clearly established empirical facts about the moral behaviour of large numbers of people who either have no place for God in their moral framework or who admit His existence but reject what they might see as the fundamentalism of divine command morality, its basis in scripture as the revealed word of God. In response to these doubts I shall make clear exactly what my argument entails, and what are its limits.

And again, notwithstanding the arguments put forward earlier concerning the possibility of alternative divine commands, the committed Christian may feel that the case I have made out is blasphemous, or verges on blasphemy, by being completely opposed to what traditional Christianity has to say about the goodness and the love of God. I have already outlined a way in which this feeling can be shown to be unjustified; and of course, if my arguments are sound then it is, strictly, unimportant whether they are blasphemous or otherwise offensive to the traditionalist's sensibility. But my concern has partly been to show that divine command theory is not merely tenable as an abstract proposition, but tenable as a Christian account of the essential nature of morality. In view of this it is worth exploring further ways of answering the doubts that may remain among those Christians who would still oppose the thesis I have presented.

The theory of divine command morality which I have defended does indeed entail that the existence of God can be inferred from the existence of any moral truth:[1] if a moral truth is wholly dependent upon God's will, if it is no more than a truth about the relationship between man's behaviour and God's intention as to what that behaviour should be, then any moral truth implies the existence of God. But what I have argued for is the rational acceptability of divine command theory rather than for its truth. I have been concerned to show that there is nothing incoherent about the theory; that arguments purporting to show that it mistakes the logic of the relationship between morality and religion are themselves mistaken; that it does not depend on a denial of the essential elements, such as personal autonomy, which any moral system must allow for, and so forth. That is to say, my argument has been, if successful, a demonstration that divine command theory could be true, not that it is true. The claim that, if it were true, it would have consequences unacceptable to atheists, is of no more than psychological interest: that a truth entails uncomfortable consequences is not a matter that counts against that truth. Then if the theory were true, an atheist would have to revise his opinion as to what was or was not acceptable, and admit the existence of God, or else deny the existence of any moral truth; he would have no other rational alternative. In any case, the argument rests squarely on important assumptions (outlined in the introduction) which the atheist would not accept.

I have also argued that divine command morality allows a reasonable role to the claims of reason in moral affairs. It has not been denied that it is possible, without either the assistance of scripture or a belief in God, to formulate a moral theory; and such a moral theory might command widespread acceptance. Rather, what I have maintained is that rationalist morality depends upon questionable assumptions concerning the ultimate goals of human activity, and that it is in general narrower in scope than one would wish were the case in any truly comprehensive moral system. If morality is to be objective, if one's ultimate goals are to be unquestionable, and if it is to be sufficiently comprehensive to allow for genuine altruism and to provide a satisfactory account of the manner in which people are to be considered equal to one another, then the rationalist's morality will be inadequate: the Christian moralist who is also a defender of divine voluntarism need not deny all moral status to the actions of the unbeliever or to the principles according which he acts, but will insist that the morality of the unbeliever cannot be enough, though it may be good as far as it goes (for it may be in accordance with the divine will even though incomplete).

The misgivings of the Christian opponent of divine voluntarism are possibly harder to allay. He may say that there must be some limits to the things God can do, or command His creatures to do, if He is to be described as loving. One would be hard put to describe as loving the actions of a parent who cruelly starved his child for years, then battered him to death; yet that sort of treatment of His creatures by God seems to be allowed for by divine voluntarism. I have argued, however, that an appreciation of the notion of divinely ordained ends, together with an understanding that God cannot be loving in the same way as that in which humans are said to be loving, can prepare the way for accepting those consequences of divine voluntarism which seem at first sight to be inconsistent with God's nature as traditionally described.[2] What has been argued is that God's commands might be *fundamentally* arbitrary. Copleston, giving Augustine's view, says that 'The laws are not arbitrary caprices of God, but their observance is willed by God, for He would not have created man without willing that man should be what He meant him to be';[3] but 'what He meant him to be' could be anything at all, arbitrarily chosen.

Further, that God could act cruelly, or command cruelty, is not to be taken as evidence that the theist's trust in His loving nature is misplaced, as has sometimes been claimed. What matters is whether He would or does act in that way. That a loving parent could act cruelly but does not is no ground for mistrust: apart from the obvious point that morally praiseworthy action presupposes a significantly free agent, it should be noted that one's trust in the love of one's parents is likely to be based on induction rather than on the conviction that they could not act otherwise. There seems to be no reason why induction should not similarly be used in justifying one's trust in God.

Perhaps the residual unease that is felt by the Christian who wishes to stress God's love rather than, as I have emphasized in my earlier arguments, His power, can be reduced if it can be partly explained as a necessary consequence of a human mode of thought: we cannot imagine a characteristic which bears no relation whatever to human ways of thinking of that characteristic - that much is trivially true. Yet we can imagine *that there be* such a characteristic. We can therefore imagine that God is loving, and in doing so imagine Him as loving in some human sense. Yet we know, given His various attributes, that our way of imagining His lovingness can not be correct. However we try to construe His love we can not depart from a humanly conceived idea of that love, though we know that to be an error. But we can imagine that there is some other way in which He is loving, though not what that is. Therefore we can imagine that whatever He should do would be loving in that unspecified and unspecifiable sense.

This rather tentative account may be less than satisfactory, but that is to be expected where what is at issue is the character of a transcendent being who is, as the tradition maintains, and as divine command theory's Christian opponents will agree, 'wholly other'. Some of the attributes traditionally ascribed to God are unproblematic, or relatively so: He is all powerful and all knowing. Others are beyond our comprehension, particularly when taken in conjunction with the more straightforward attributes. It should therefore be a matter of agreement among all Christians that there is a serious problem in understanding what it is for a divine being to be all loving, if this is understood in any sense other than that suggested earlier: God ordains certain ends for man, then provides the means for man to achieve those ends.[4]

If the principal objection to divine voluntarism is that it entails something which is inconsistent with God's being all loving, yet it is impossible to give any greater content to His all lovingness than that suggested, then this objection is weakened so much that it becomes little more than a feeling of unease, which can itself be accounted for by recalling that man necessarily thinks in certain ways.

It follows, too, from what I have argued, that there is a sense in which God could have been other than He is said to be on the Christian account; but this need not be thought of as being opposed to the tradition. God could have done what He has not done; He could have ordered morality differently; He could have commanded things which were very different from those that He has, according to the tradition, actually commanded; His Word, the Logos, in so far as it embodies moral truth, could have been different: then, to the extent that His nature is to be identified with the Word, or with what He has done, He could have been what He is not. It is true that Christians hold the Logos to have been 'begotten' not 'created'; but that should not be taken to entail that it could never have been different, for it could have been eternally begotten with characteristics different from those which tradition ascribes to it. Clark says that the Logos's having been begotten means that 'the One could not ever have produced any other word but Love, that there could not ever have been another pattern to be our lode-star'.[5] But it was Arius's mistake, countered by the council of Nicaea's affirmation that the Son of God is 'begotten, not made', to suppose the Son to be a creature of the Father rather than consubstantial with Him, to assert the Son's temporal nature rather than His eternity; his mistake was not to suppose that the Logos could have been different. The two issues are separate.

There are reasons why one might want to oppose the tendency, implicit in much Christian thought and made explicit in divine command theory, to take scripture literally when possible. Saint Paul's words, 'the letter killeth, but the spirit giveth life'[6] are sometimes quoted in support of a position of leniency with regard to the literal, scriptural precepts of the moral law, and in support of an anti-literalist, anti-fundamentalist interpretation of scripture generally; for it is felt that an excessively literal reading of scripture is simply not sustainable, particularly in the light of modern scientific knowledge.[7] However, as I have argued, the difficulties for the Christian either of adopting a wholly non literal interpretation or of relying upon a reading of scripture which takes some middle way, accepting some parts of it as literally true while discarding other parts which are not obviously symbolic or in plain contradiction of certain facts, are quite grave. Cupitt has argued that

> Ordinary folk may think mythologically that their religious beliefs express timeless and objective truths, but specialists know that every last detail of every religion is human, evolved in human societies and having a purely human history that can in principle be reconstructed... All meaning and truth and value are man made and could not be otherwise.[8]

Quite apart from the philosophical problems entailed by that position, it is clearly an approach to Christianity which is incompatible with the tradition. Yet if one proposes a compromise in order to reject as non literal those claims in scripture which seem embarrassing to some modern minds, one risks either the denial of an important core truth of Christianity or confusion.[9] As Charlton says, such compromise positions are very difficult to sustain: 'There are no satisfactory principles of criticism by which we can accept the testimony of the Gospels to one supernatural occurrence but not to another'.[10] The rejection of literalism can sometimes raise more difficulties than it is meant to avoid.[11]

Besides, that aspect of fundamentalism that can be characterized as literalism is by no means absurd. It is worth remarking that literalism was once the norm in Christian circles. It has never, of course, been a universally adopted approach; but as Clark points out, it is unprofitable 'to imagine that our predecessors, even when they were mistaken, were fools'.[12] There are other reasons for accepting literalism than ignorance or unintelligent and unreflective acceptance of what one has been told. There are, for instance, other ways of reconciling the account of Abraham and Isaac with God's love than by doubting the literal truth of the story, given that we can know both a priori and empirically that God's love is not like our love. Literalism is out of fashion, but it is much more defensible than fashion supposes, particularly in the context of a religion which claims and, I have argued, requires revelational support. It is true that some branches of the Christian tradition have emphasized the importance of sources of information other than scripture; but they do not thereby dispense with the need to depend upon the revealed texts. Tugwell writes that

> Both Barnabas and the Didachist are convinced that, through Christ, God has revealed his will and his truth to us, he has shown us the 'way of life'. But this revelation is not a lump sum on which we can presume. The word of God has to be cultivated;[13]

but the cultivation of the word depends upon knowing what it is. 'There is a great book: the very appearance of created things';[14] but we do not know how to interpret it without the rules laid down in the other Book.

It is difficult to sustain the position which, in terms of their literal truth, admits the Resurrection but denies the flood; which admits the Incarnation but denies the stone tablets; which admits the Redemption but denies Eden. The criterion which is being used here is not one that modern science has produced. The temptation to explain away, as if these things were a barrier to faith, the awkward, the strange and the miraculous, should be resisted. Such an approach seems far more likely to result either in bafflement at its inconsistency or in complete loss of faith. The currently accepted account of human origins (to take an example which has been controversial) is well known, but neo-Darwinian evolution is not the only logically possible account. One needs only to reflect on Gosse's suggested explanation of fossils[15] to appreciate that creationism is as consistent with the facts as is evolutionism: had there been a real Adam, and had he felled a tree, he would no doubt have discovered tree rings inside it. Any creation would necessarily carry within itself the false illusion of past duration. Each of the rival theories 'saves the phenomena' equally well. This point, like Gosse's own account, is not intended as any sort of argument in favour of creationism; what Gosse shows is that *if* the world was created in the manner described in the book of Genesis, we should not be surprised to find that it has the features which it has actually got, fossils included. The truth or falsity of the literalist's account is not the issue here: what is clear is that it is unjustifiable to criticize that account as scientifically naive or ignorant.

Just as there are incidents described in scripture which, while not irrational, nevertheless require that a believer should go beyond the rational, so there are scriptural precepts which Christians must accept but which are not rationally discoverable. Reason is never contravened, but is not sufficient, without revelation, to support a Christian view either of correct behaviour or of the nature of God and the world. What has reason to say about the justice and fairness of the treatment of the eleventh hour *arriviste*[16] or about the equity of our comparison to the potter's clay?[17] What has secular, rationalist morality to tell us about Christ's mission being not to bring peace but the sword?[18] What is a logically minded rationalist to make of the apparent disregard of the law of identity which allows us to say that God has no body, and Christ has a body, and Christ is God? There are instances of scriptural commands which Christians are not able to obey by applying what they take to be the spirit of law, because they have nothing to go on but the letter, and they can not neglect it, or interpret it, or apply the doctrine of *epikeia*, on pain of inconsistency.

Literalism's dogmas need be no less scientific, no more open to rational refutation, no more intrinsically unlikely (is there any relevant criterion of intrinsic probability?) than either opposing claims which are currently popular in terms of their scientific acceptance or the essential beliefs held in common by all Christians, whatever their attitude to the letter of the text.

In the matter of autonomy, submitting to God's commands is not the same thing as abandoning self rule, in the sense intended by the critics of a morality which is based on obedience. On his conversion to Roman Catholicism, Oursler found himself accused of having become, intellectually, a serf.[19] But the position of the obedient believer is not like that; rather, it is like that referred to by the Psalmist: he rules himself after God's word.[20] He obeys God's word, it is true; but he still rules himself - he chooses to obey. There remain things that he is not free to choose, but that is a consequence of there being objective truths, including objective moral truths. The Psalmist asks, 'Make me to go in the path of thy commandments, for that is my desire';[21] and if his prayer is granted, his autonomy is untouched.

Is the outcome of my arguments not a divine *will* theory rather than a divine *command* theory? Should not the answer to the question posed at the beginning of the introduction be 'Because God so wills'? In a sense, it is a divine will theory;

nevertheless, divine commands are fundamental. This is so not only because we cannot infer God's will without knowledge of His commands, nor simply because His commands are a direct expression of His will, and not just an epistemological aid. God wills many things, no doubt, which do not give rise to creaturely obligations. But what He wills in relation to our behaviour constitutes an imperative. In the absence of His commands, certain obligations would no longer exist. And if, as I have suggested, the most important feature of morally good behaviour is not the nature of that behaviour in itself, but its nature as obedience, then clearly divine commands are basic. Further, it is possible that the Christian duty to love God is satisfied by obedience to Him. Christians are not called upon to adopt any particular emotional attitude to Him, nor to look after Him, worry about His future, and so forth. They are called upon to obey Him, to defer to Him, to acknowledge Him for what He is. The greatest sin is, in the tradition, pride; and that can be viewed as consisting primarily in disobedience - it amounts to the attempted elevation of the creature to a position he cannot hold, by way of the refusal to conform his will to the divine will. That is disobedience. Far from morality having nothing to do with obedience, it could be about nothing else but obedience.

Notes

1 Cf. Quinn (1970), *Divine Commands and Moral Requirements*, Clarendon Press: Oxford, p. 61.
2 When Fisher, rejecting divine voluntarism, compares morality to a car manual, in which the manufacturer's instructions are determined by the facts, reflecting the correct way to care for and operate the car, he ignores God's role in determining ends. Just as a car could be a suicide machine with ornamental extras, in which case it might be 'correct' to loosen the wheel nuts before driving, so will the rules of the moral code depend on what man's purpose is, as ordained by God. See: Fisher (1990), 'Because God Says So', in Beaty, *Christian Theism and the Problems of Philosophy*, University of Notre Dame Press: Notre Dame, pp. 361-2.
3 Copleston (1954), *A History of Philosophy*, vol. 2, Burns Oates and Washbourne: London, p. 83.
4 In this context, it would perhaps be possible to develop the suggestions on divine love made by Sayers. She sees it as essentially creative, 'the Energy of creation', neither sentimental nor possessive. See Sayers (1994), *The Mind of The Maker*, Mowbray: London, pp. 104-9.
5 Clark (1986), *The Mysteries of Religion*, Blackwell: Oxford, pp. 98-9.
6 2 Cor. 3:6.
7 The resistance to fundamentalism is sometimes expressed in stronger terms, and on other grounds: 'A fundamentalist is... one who professes

belief in a creed, doctrine, dogma, code, or ideology that he accepts unreservedly and without question. His commitment is firm, inflexible, and unwavering. These principles are taken as absolute, unchanging, eternal. The system of fundamentalist belief, at least in theory if not in practice, is used as a guide for all aspects of life and encourages the development of a pathological authoritarian personality' - Kurtz (1988), 'The Growth of Fundamentalism Worldwide', in The Academy of Humanism's *Neo-Fundamentalism: The Humanist Response*, Buffalo, New York, p. 11.

8   Cupitt (1984), *The Sea of Faith*, BBC: London, pp. 19-20.
9   I develop this point further in (1995), 'Literalism and Tolerance', *New Blackfriars*.
10 Charlton (1988), *Philosophy and Christian Belief*, Sheed and Ward: London, pp. 98-9.
11 Cf. the view of the American politician William Jennings Bryan, given in Marty and Appleby (1992), *The Glory and The Power: the Fundamentalist Challenge to the Modern World*, Boston, Massachusetts, p. 62: '[He] was to say, after hearing all the right doctrines in the creeds of moderate churches but finding the reciters of creeds referring to their attachments as 'symbolic' or 'spiritual' or 'sacramental', that such attachments meant the sucking of truth out of every doctrine, that only literalism could save it'.
12 Clark, op. cit., p. ix.
13 Tugwell (1984), *Ways of Imperfection: An Exploration of Christian Spirituality*, Darton, Longman and Todd: London, p. 5.
14 Augustine, *Sermo Mai*, 126, 6.
15 Gosse (1857), *Omphalos: An Attempt to Untie the Geological Knot*, London.
16 Matthew 20:1-15.
17 Isaiah 45:9.
18 Matthew 10:34.
19 Oursler (1950), 'The Greatest Thing in My Life', in O'Brien, *The Road to Damascus*, vol. 1, W.H. Allen: London, pp. 17-26.
20 Ps. 119:9, in the translation in the Book of Common Prayer.
21 Ps. 119:35 - Book of Common Prayer.

Bibliography

Abelard, P. (1971), *Ethics*, Luscombe, D.E. (ed.), Oxford University Press: Oxford.
Abraham, W.J. and Holtzer, S.W. (1987), *The Rationality of Religious Belief*, Oxford University Press: Oxford.
Adams, R.M. (1987), *The Virtue of Faith*, Oxford University Press: Oxford.
Anscombe, G.E.M. (1958), 'Modern Moral Philosophy', *Philosophy* 33, pp. 1-19.
Attfield, R. (1978), *God and the Secular*, Cardiff.
Bambrough, R. (1979), *Moral Scepticism and Moral Knowledge*, London.
Barth, K. (1957), *Church Dogmatics*, Edinburgh.
Battaglia, A. (1981), *Toward a Reformulation of Natural Law*, New York.
Beaty, M.D. (1990), *Christian Theism and the Problems of Philosophy*, University of Notre Dame Press: Notre Dame.
Berkeley, G. (1955), 'On The Will of God', in *Works*, vol. 7, London.
Brody, B.A. (1981), 'Morality and Religion Reconsidered', in Helm (1981).
Brown, C. (1968), *Philosophy and the Christian Faith*, London.
Brown, P. (1968), 'Religious Morality: A Reply to Flew and Campbell', *Mind* 77, pp. 577-80.
Brown, R.F. (1991), 'God's Ability to Will Moral Evil', *Faith and Philosophy* 8, pp. 3-20.
Brunner, E. (1961), *The Divine Imperative*, Lutterworth Press: London.
Butler, J. (1900), *The Analogy of Religion*, London.
Card, Orson Scott (1991), *Xenocide*, London.
Catechism of the Catholic Church (1994), Vatican.
Chandler, J. (1985), 'Clark on God's Law and Morality', *Philosophical Quarterly* 35, pp. 87-90.
Charlton, W. (1988), *Philosophy and Christian Belief*, Sheed and Ward: London.
Chesterton, G.K. (1933), *St. Thomas Aquinas*, London.

Clark, S.R.L. (1987), 'God's Law and Chandler', *Philosophical Quarterly* 37, pp. 203-8.
Clark, S.R.L. (1982), 'God's Law and Morality', *Philosophical Quarterly* 32, pp. 339-47.
Clark, S.R.L. (1986), *The Mysteries of Religion*, Blackwell: Oxford.
Clouser, R. (1983), 'Religious Language: A New Look at an Old Problem', in Van der Hoeven and Wolterstorff (eds), *Rationality in the Calvinian Tradition*, University Press of America.
Copleston, F.C. (1954), *A History of Philosophy*, Burns Oates and Washbourne: London.
Copleston, F.C. (1986), *Aquinas*, Penguin Books: London.
Cudworth, R. (1731), *Treatise Concerning Eternal and Immutable Morality*, London; facsimile reprint (1976), Garland: New York.
Cupitt, D. (1984), *The Sea of Faith*, BBC: London.
Daly, G. (1991), 'Conscience, Guilt and Sin', in Freyne (1991).
de Graaff, G. (1966), 'God and Morality', in Ramsey (1966).
Dedek, J. (1979), 'Intrinsically Evil Acts: An Historical Study of the Mind of St. Thomas', *The Thomist* 43, pp. 385-413.
Dedek, J. (1983), 'Intrinsically Evil Acts: The Emergence of a Doctrine', *Recherches de Theologie Ancienne et Medievale* 50, pp. 191-226.
Descartes, R. (1970), *Philosophical Letters*, trans. Kenny, A., Oxford.
Donagan, A. (1977), *The Theory of Morality*, Chicago.
Donovan, P. (1976), *Religious Language*, Sheldon Press: London.
Douglas, M. (1979), *Purity and Danger*, London.
Duns Scotus (1891-5), 'Quaestiones in Libros Sententiarum', in *Works*, Paris.
Dussel, E. (1988), *Ethics and Community*, Burns and Oates.
Dworkin, G. (1988), *The Theory and Practice of Autonomy*, Cambridge University Press: Cambridge.
Edwards, J. (1970), *Works*, Holbrook, C.A. (ed.), Yale.
Ewing, A.C. (1961), 'The Autonomy of Ethics', in Ramsey (1961).
Faber, P. (1985), 'The Euthyphro Objection to Divine Normative Theories: A Response', *Religious Studies* 21, pp. 559-72.
Farrell, W. (1939), *A Companion to the Summa*, London.
Fisher, C. (1990), 'Because God Says So', in Beaty (1990).
Flint, T.P. and Freddoso, A.J. (1987), 'Maximal Power', in Morris (1987).
Frankena, W.K. (1981), 'Is Morality Logically Dependent on Religion?', in Helm (1981).
Freyne, S. (1991), *Ethics and The Christian*, Columba Press: Dublin.
Garnett, A.C. (1955), *Religion and the Moral Life*, New York.
Gascoigne, R. (1985), 'God and Objective Moral Values', *Religious Studies* 21, pp. 531-49.
Geach, P. (1977), *Providence and Evil*, Cambridge.
Geach, P. (1981), 'The Moral Law and The Law of God', in Helm (1981).

Gewirth, A. (1978), *Reason and Morality*, University of Chicago Press.
Goldstick, D. (1990), 'Could God make a Contradiction True?', *Religious Studies* 26, pp. 377-87.
Goldstick, D. (1974), 'Monotheism's Euthyphro Problem', *Canadian Journal of Philosophy* 3, pp. 585-9.
Gosse, P. (1857), *Omphalos: An Attempt to Untie the Geological Knot*, London.
Gunton, C. (1993), *The One, The Three and The Many*, Cambridge.
Hamel, E. (1964), *Loi Naturelle et Loi du Christ*, Desclee de Brouwer: Paris.
Hare, R.M. (1963), *Freedom and Reason*, Oxford University Press: Oxford.
Hart, H.L.A. (1961), *The Concept of Law*, Oxford.
Helm, P. (1981), *Divine Commands and Morality*, Oxford University Press: Oxford.
Henry, C.F.H. (1957), *Christian Personal Ethics*, Grand Rapids, Michigan.
Hick, J. (1990), 'Soul-Making and Suffering', in Adams, M.M. and R.M. (eds), *The Problem of Evil*, Oxford.
Idziak, J.M. (1979), *Divine Command Morality: Historical and Contemporary Readings*, Edwin Mellen Press: New York.
John Paul II (1993), *Veritatis Splendor*, Vatican.
Johnson, P. (1990), *A History of Christianity*, Penguin Books: London.
Keneally, T. (1982), *Schindler's Ark*, London.
Kenny, A. (1988), *The God of the Philosophers*, Oxford.
Kierkegaard, S. (1985), *Fear and Trembling*, Penguin Books: London.
Kretzmann, N. (1983), 'Abraham, Isaac and Euthyphro: God and the Basis of Morality', in Stump, D.V. (1983), *Hamartia: The Concept of Error in the Western Tradition*, New York.
Kurtz, P. (1988), 'The Growth of Fundamentalism Worldwide', in The Academy of Humanism's *Neo-Fundamentalism: The Humanist Response*, Buffalo, New York.
Kvanvig, J. and McCann, H. (1988), 'Divine Conservation and the Persistence of the World', in Morris (1988).
Leslie, J. (1978), 'Efforts to Explain All Existence', *Mind* 87, pp. 181-94.
Leslie, J. (1980), 'The World's Necessary Existence', *International Journal for the Philosophy of Religion* 11, pp. 207-24.
Leslie, J. (1979), *Value and Existence*, Oxford.
Lewis, C.S. (1988), *The Problem of Pain*, Fount Paperbacks.
Locke, D. (1981), 'The Principle of Equal Interests', *Philosophical Review* 90, pp. 531-59.
MacDonald, S. (1990), 'Egoistic Rationalism: Aquinas's Basis for Christian Morality', in Beaty (1990).
MacIntyre, A. (1981), *After Virtue*, Duckworth: London.
Mackie, J.L. (1955), 'Evil and Omnipotence', *Mind* 64, pp. 200-12.
Mackie, J.L. (1982), *The Miracle of Theism*, Oxford.
MacNamara, V. (1991), 'Ethics Human and Christian', in Freyne (1991).

Mahoney, J. (1968), 'Obedience: Consent or Conformity?', *The Way*, supplement no. 6, pp. 5-19.
Mahoney, J. (1987), *The Making of Moral Theology*, Oxford.
Mann, W.E. (1991), 'The Best of All Possible Worlds', in MacDonald, S. (1991), *Being and Goodness*, Cornell University Press: Ithaca, New York.
Marty, M.E. and Appleby, R.S. (1992), *The Glory and The Power: the Fundamentalist Challenge to the Modern World*, Boston, Massachusetts.
Mayes, A.D.H. (1991), 'The Decalogue of Moses: An Enduring Ethical Programme?', in Freyne (1991).
McCabe, H. (1980), 'God II: Freedom', *New Blackfriars*, pp. 456-69.
Meynell, H. (1994), *Is Christianity True?*, London.
Meynell, H. (1972), 'The Euthyphro Dilemma', *Proceedings of the Aristotelian Society*, supplementary volume, pp. 223-34.
Mitchell, B. (1980), *Morality: Religious and Secular*, Oxford University Press: Oxford.
Moore, G.E. (1903), *Principia Ethica*, Cambridge University Press: Cambridge.
Morris, T.V. (1988), *Divine and Human Action*, Cornell University Press: Ithaca, New York.
Morris, T.V. (1985), 'On God and Mann: A View of Divine Simplicity', *Religious Studies* 21, pp. 299-318.
Morris, T.V. (1987), *The Concept of God*, Oxford University Press: Oxford.
Morris, T.V. and Menzel, C. (1986), 'Absolute Creation', *American Philosophical Quarterly* 23, pp. 353-62.
Moser, M. and Leers, B. (1990), *Moral Theology*, Burns and Oates.
Mouw, R. (1990), *The God Who Commands*, University of Notre Dame Press.
Muirhead, J.H. (1931), *The Platonic Tradition*, London.
Murdoch, I. (1993), *Metaphysics as a Guide to Morals*, Penguin Books: London.
Murray, J.C. (1964), *The Problem of God*, Yale University Press.
Nelson, D.M. (1992), *The Priority of Prudence: Virtue and Natural Law in Thomas Aquinas and The Implications for Modern Ethics*, Pennsylvania State University Press: Pennsylvania.
Nielsen, K. (1973), *Ethics Without God*, London.
Nielsen, K. (1985), *Philosophy and Atheism*, New York.
Nowell-Smith, P.H. (1966), 'Morality: Religious and Secular', in Ramsey (1966).
Oakes, R.A. (1972), 'Reply to Professor Rachels', *Religious Studies* 8, pp. 165-7.
Ockham, W. (1495), *Super Quattuor Libros Sententiarum*, in *Opera Plurima*, vols. 3 and 4, Lyons; facsimile reprint (1962), Gregg Press: London.
O'Connor, D.J. (1967), *Aquinas and Natural Law*, London.
O'Donovan, O. (1987), 'The Reasonable Man: An Appreciation', in Abraham, W.J. and Holtzer, S.W. (1987).
Oursler, F. (1950), 'The Greatest Thing in My Life', in O'Brien, J.A. (1950), *The Road to Damascus*, vol. 1, W.H. Allen: London, pp. 17-26.

Paley, William (1785), *The Principles of Moral and Political Philosophy*, London.
Parkinson, G.H.R. (1988), *Leibniz: Philosophical Writings*, Dent and Sons: London.
Paton, H.J. (1987), *The Moral Law*, London.
Pearl, L. (1986), 'The Misuse of Anselm's Formula for God's Perfection', *Religious Studies* 22, pp. 355-65.
Phillips, D.Z. (1966), 'God and Ought', in Ramsey (1966).
Pike, N. (1969), 'Omnipotence and God's Ability to Sin', *American Philosophical Quarterly* 6, pp. 208-16.
Pirsig, R.M. (1991), *Lila: An Inquiry Into Morals*, London.
Plantinga, A. (1967), *God and Other Minds*, Ithaca.
Poole, R. (1991), *Morality and Modernity*, London.
Potts, T.C. (1980), *Conscience in Medieval Philosophy*, Cambridge University Press: Cambridge.
Price, R. (1974), *A Review of the Principal Questions in Morals*, Raphael, D D (ed.), Oxford.
Quinn, P.L. (1990), 'An Argument for Divine Command Ethics', in Beaty (1990).
Quinn, P.L. (1978), *Divine Commands and Moral Requirements*, Clarendon Press: Oxford.
Quinn, P.L. (1983), 'Divine Conservation, Continuous Creation, and Human Action', in Freddoso, A.J. (1983), *The Existence and Nature of God*, University of Notre Dame Press.
Quinn, P.L. (1990), 'The Recent Revival of Divine Command Ethics', *Philosophy and Phenomenological Research*, pp. 345-65.
Rachels, J. (1971), 'God and Human Attitudes', *Religious Studies* 7, pp. 325-37.
Radice, B. (1968), *Early Christian Writings*, Penguin Books: London.
Ramsey, I.T. (1966), *Christian Ethics and Contemporary Philosophy*, London.
Ramsey, I.T.(1961), *Prospect for Metaphysics*, London.
Rickaby, J. (1892), *Moral Philosophy*, London.
Rooney, P.V. (1995), 'Divine Commands and Arbitrariness', *Religious Studies* 31, pp. 149-65.
Rooney, P.V. (1996), 'Divine Commands, Christian Platonism and God's Nature', *Heythrop Journal* 37, pp. 155-75.
Rooney, P.V. (1995), 'Divine Commands, Natural Law and Aquinas', *Scottish Journal of Religious Studies* 16, pp. 117-40.
Rooney, P.V. (1995), 'Literalism and Tolerance', *New Blackfriars* 76, pp. 542-5.
Sacks, J. (1991), *The Persistence of Faith*, London.
Sayers, D.L. (1994), *The Mind of The Maker*, Mowbray: London.
Searle, J.R. (1964), 'How to Derive *Ought* from *Is*', *Philosophical Review* 73, pp. 43-58.
Simon, Y. (1967), *The Tradition of Natural Law*, New York.

Sokol, M.Z. (1986), 'The Autonomy of Reason, Revealed Morality and Jewish Law', *Religious Studies* 22, pp. 423-37.
Stump, E. and Kretzmann, N. (1988), 'Being and Goodness', in Morris (1988).
Suarez, F. (1944), *De Legibus*, London.
Sullivan, S.J. (1993), 'Arbitrariness, Divine Commands, and Morality', *Philosophy of Religion* 33, pp. 33-45.
Swinburne, R.G. (1974), 'Duty and the Will of God', *Canadian Journal of Philosophy* 4, pp. 213-27.
Swinburne, R.G. (1973), 'Omnipotence', *American Philosophical Quarterly* 10, pp. 231-37.
Swinburne, R.G. (1977), *The Coherence of Theism*, Oxford.
Swinburne, R.G. (1979), *The Existence of God*, Oxford.
Tugwell, S. (1984), *Ways of Imperfection: An Exploration of Christian Spirituality*, Darton, Longman and Todd: London.
Unamuno, Miguel de (1921), *The Tragic Sense of Life in Men and in Peoples*, London.
Van den Brink, G. (1992), *Almighty God: A Study of the Doctrine of Divine Omnipotence*, Utrecht.
Wernham, J.C.S. (1968), *Two Russian Thinkers*, Toronto.
Wierenga, E.R. (1983), 'A Defensible Divine Command Theory', *Nous* 17, pp. 387-407.
Wierenga, E.R. (1989), *The Nature of God*, Cornell University Press: Ithaca, New York.
Williams, B. (1972), *Morality: An Introduction to Ethics*, Cambridge University Press: Cambridge.
Wilson, B.R. (1970), *Rationality*, Oxford.
Wolfson, H.A. (1961), *Religious Philosophy*, Cambridge, Mass.
Wolfson, H.A. (1970), *The Philosophy of the Church Fathers*, Cambridge, Mass.
Wolterstorff, N. (1986), 'The Migration of Theistic Arguments: From Natural Theology to Evidentialist Apologetics', in Audi, R. and Wainwright, W.J. (1986), *Rationality, Religious Belief, and Moral Commitment*, Cornell University Press: Ithaca, New York.
Woods, G.F. (1966), *A Defence of Theological Ethics*, Cambridge University Press: Cambridge.
Yandell, K.E. (1988), 'Divine Necessity and Divine Goodness', in Morris (1988).
Young, R. (1986), *Personal Autonomy*, London.